Ascent to Love

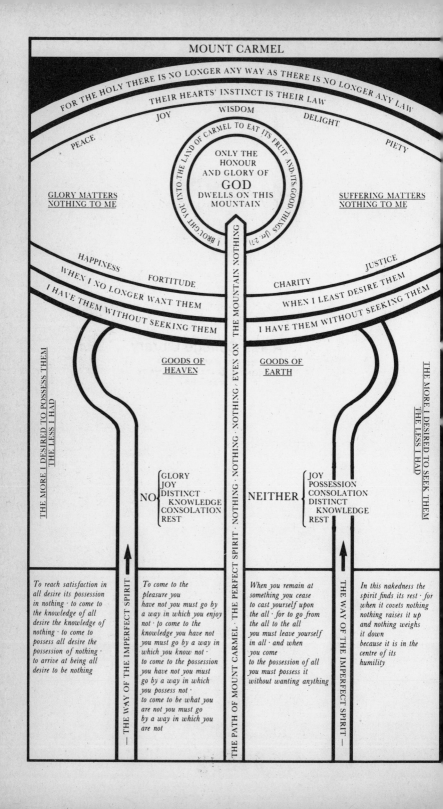

Ascent to Love

The Spiritual Teaching of
St John of the Cross

RUTH BURROWS

Dimension Books Inc.
Denville, N.J. 07834

First U.S.A. edition by Dimension Books Inc.
P.O. Box 811, Denville, N.J. 07834 through
arrangement with Darton, Longman and Todd Ltd, London

ISBN 0–87193–258–X

Phototypeset by
Input Typesetting Ltd,
London SW19 8DR
Printed and bound in Great Britain by
Anchor Brendon Ltd, Tiptree, Essex

Contents

Acknowledgements

I acknowledge my debt to the great Karl Rahner. Those who are familiar with his writings will recognise his influence. This study of John of the Cross is, I feel, a collective work, many people have contributed to it whether they know it or not. In the first place there is my own community, and here I must include those with whom I have shared my life for many years but who are now in the Carmels of Sclerder and Walsingham. Our life together has been the matrix of my insights. I thank one and all. In particular I thank those who read through my early drafts and offered comments and criticisms which have proved invaluable. I thank those who have permitted me to quote them directly and those whose thoughts I have borrowed as life in common allows. There are others outside the community to whom my thanks go. They are likely to be too humble to think they have offered anything, but I know my debt to them and so does God.

I thank Sister Elizabeth Ruth for her devoted and meticulous work in preparing my typescript for the publishers and thereby lifting a burden off me. And lastly I thank Father Michael Edwards for allowing Sister Elizabeth Ruth to base the frontispiece on his photograph of the Beas copy of St John of the Cross's drawing of the Mount.

R.B.

Eve of the Feast of
Our Lady of Mount Carmel
15 July 1986

Note

Unless otherwise stated the longer portions of Scripture are the author's own rendering. The references from John of the Cross are likewise the author's own, based on the David Lewis edition of the *Complete Works*.

Introduction

It is no coincidence that the order of Carmel has produced three major authorities on the lived experience of the fulness of the Christian life – St Teresa, St John of the Cross and St Thérèse of Lisieux. Each has given the world a unique presentation of what the gospel, the good news, is all about; and its essence, in the Carmelite tradition as well as in the earlier ones from which it derives, is called mystical union.

The Order of Carmel stands for the mystical. Everything in its teaching and way of life as established by St Teresa is directed precisely towards this. A full flowering of the mystical life and the Christian life are one and the same thing. The culmination, perfection, fulfilment of the Christian life – 'all that the Lord has promised' – is, in our special terminology, the mystical marriage or transforming union. The ascent of Mount Carmel is but the fulness of the Christian life, which is synonymous with the fulness of human being. There are not two vocations, one to human fulfilment and the other, if we are special and privileged, to Christian fulfilment. There is only *one* fulfilment to be achieved either in this world or the next, that which we call mystical marriage or transforming union.

This is essentially what Carmel means to me. It is a view of human life translated into a definite purpose and aim. Climbing a mountain to meet God? Yes. But the mountain itself is God and he cannot be scaled by merely human endeavour. What Carmel does is to disengage the bare components of the human vocation, what is really involved in being human, and tries to live them in an absolute, naked

1

sort of way. So convinced am I that Carmel is nothing other than a living out in a stark manner what is the very essence of the human vocation that, were I to come across any practice, ideal, principle, which has not its correlative in life 'outside' it would be jettisoned as unauthentic. There is a distinction to be made between living Carmel and living in Carmel, just as there is between being a Christian and practising the Christian religion. It is the former that matters, and the latter is useless unless it leads to the primary goal.

Our three great writers belong to the world, they are catholic, timeless in the core of their teaching. This little book is concerned with John of the Cross and seeks to show the importance of his doctrine. Many times I have been pressed to write something on John: 'Do for him what you have done for Teresa, put him in modern dress for us.' Only recently have I been able to explain to myself the reluctance I have felt to tackle such a work. It is certainly not due to lack of appreciation, on the contrary his doctrine has been a beacon to me. I have long recognised that he has a message for us which, as he himself asserts, is the more necessary the less it is desired, welcomed or understood. His message is the clean opposite of the wisdom of this world – as we should expect if it is the message of Jesus. I am loath to put John's works into the hands of the inexperienced for I have seen the harm done through misunderstanding what he says. There are those who misread him, finding him forbidding, inhuman, unchristian. Thus they cast him aside, depriving themselves of his Christ-wisdom. Others do not question John's authority but, being anxious and spiritually insecure, not yet knowing where God is, compulsively undertake an unbalanced inhuman asceticism, thinking that this is what he is advocating.

I myself used to read John with a sinking heart, fascinated indeed (for who could fail to see that here was one who had, so to speak, pierced the veil and really seen God) but stricken with dismay at what he appeared to be demanding. Indeed he seemed to assume that what he asked was wholly practicable for a generous heart, while to me it seemed impossible. Gradually however I came to understand, and I now recognise in what he says the call of the beloved to all who want him – he whose yoke is sweet and whose burden is light.

Hence my reluctance springs from the fact that there is in John a disturbing contradiction. For me his authentic teaching is summed up succinctly in his drawing of the mount and expounded principally in the *Ascent of Mount Carmel* and the *Dark Night*. It is to be found too in his letters, maxims and counsels, and a careful reading reveals it underlying the *Spiritual Canticle* and the *Living Flame*. However it is in these two latter works that we find the inconsistency. Look at the drawing of the mount (frontispiece). See the road straight as the drive of an arrow to the summit, a summit lost in mystery. It is a way of Nothing, *'and on the mountain nothing'*. How powerful the silence! Now read the *Canticle* and the *Living Flame* with their flamboyant descriptions of what the perfect or near-perfect actually experience. These works seem to belie the truth of John's fundamental teaching. He would have us detached from spiritual riches certainly, but he seems to be saying here, 'detach yourselves from crude consolations so that one day you can enjoy something immensely superior even in this life'. I deliberately say 'seems'. It is tempting to speculate, to advance theories for this apparently blatant inconsistency but that would not serve the purpose of this book. It is enough to remark that for the majority of readers the impression is such as I have given. If John is *really* saying what these people *think* he is then we are justified in disregarding him in given instances. Take for example his description of the death of the perfect which purports to be attended by marvellous sweetness and consolation far surpassing all they have experienced during the course of their life.[1] They die in 'delicious ecstasy'. Well, we have only to turn to Jesus in the Gospel of Mark and the Epistle to the Hebrews to see that this cannot be true at its face value. Elsewhere John claims that the perfect no longer experience natural emotions, not even compassion, though God sometimes for special reasons allows his holy ones to know such emotion, as in the

---

[1]See *Living Flame*, st. 1, v. 6.

case of the Blessed Virgin and St Paul.[1] Need we comment? What of Jesus himself weeping over Jerusalem and at the tomb of Lazurus? Moved with compassion before a disconsolate widow carrying her dead son to the grave? Showing anger and frustration and shuddering dread.

On the other hand John is an utterly safe guide for the beginner, and I use the word here as John himself sometimes uses it, referring to those who have begun to enter into the mystical dimension, those who have begun the ascent of Mount Carmel and are moving up its face. The Prologue to the *Ascent* expresses his purpose very clearly; it is the fundamental insight which is his own unique contribution to the mystical tradition. He wants to explain the experience he calls the 'dark night' through which souls must pass on their way to the light of divine union. He wants to show beginners, as well as those who have made some progress, how to resign themselves into God's hands when it is his good pleasure to take control. Readily it is assumed that the path of contemplation will be sunlit, unambiguous. Not so, says John. It is a path beset with trouble, distress, temptation; it is obscure, bewildering. Few interpret the way aright and reliable guides are rare. He is aware of the truth and importance of his own insights if beginners are to reach the end of the journey. Many set out and make progress but very few go far, and one of the principle reasons, says John, is lack of proper guidance. This he sets out to give.

The perfect need no guide. What good do they do us, these attempts to draw aside the curtain from the mystery of the summit? All we need to know is *how to get there*. Show us the way and let the end look after itself! Follow the way and we shall surely reach the goal and know for ourselves with true knowledge. This is consistent with Jesus' teaching. He never attempted to tell us what heaven was like; rather he devoted himself to showing us how to live our lives in perfect obedience to the Father here and now, with the absolute assurance of a blessed consummation.

[1] *Canticle*, st. 21.

If we want a concrete illustration of John's doctrine carried consistently to its end we shall find it in the Carmelite Thérèse of Lisieux. She knew John of the Cross and loved him well, especially at a particular period of her life when, together with the Scriptures, his writings were her only spiritual food. At the end of her life someone drew her attention to John's grandiloquent descriptions of the perfect, how they see their own beauty: 'Beauty? I see no beauty, only a poor creature to whom God has been infinitely good.' Thérèse experienced herself as poor and imperfect; faced with John's 'delicious ecstasy' she points to Jesus on the cross. 'Our Lord died in anguish undoubtedly and yet his death is the most beautiful the world has known. To die of love is not to die in ecstasy.'

Of course Thérèse and John are both trying to describe something which cannot be described. A characteristic of the state of spiritual marriage is that it is different, absolutely, from all that has gone before it. It is incommunicable and remains the individual's lived experience for which there are no words, no ideas. Let an attempt be made to describe it and inevitably it is put within the range of the familiar. A gulf lies between the spiritual marriage and anything that can be remotely touched upon in word and image. One mystic may express his or her experience as anguish, another as joy. We could point to passages in John which would seem to contradict that the summits of the spiritual life are beyond suffering; just as we can recall Thérèse's claim that she could no longer suffer because all suffering had become sweet to her. Joy and transport were certainly in her depths but in a way that still left her a prey to physical and mental agony. Indeed both our saints saw love as the only reward of love; neither was interested in attaining anything, getting anything for themselves. They wanted to surrender to love, to allow love to have its way with them to the full, and thus give love for love. Theirs was a completely selfless aim.

John, it seems to me, has given us, as no one else, the absolutes of the spiritual life, the bedrock principles, the 'musts' deriving from who and what God is and what we are. His basic teaching – and this is my sole concern – cannot be dismissed as one way among many. The power and authority of John lie precisely in that what he has laid bare for us is the *sine qua non* of it all, grounded on the reality of God and the reality of man. His manner of presentation, language, patterns of thought, are relative, yet all too often they get in the way and impair the unimpeachable truth of what he is saying. The core of John is nothing other than a stark presentation of the heart of the gospel. His doctrine is now the church's heritage but in his own times it was a major breakthrough. It is not that he revealed things unknown before but he was the first to make an authoritative, scientific analysis of them. He *shows* us the foundations that had already been established and the relation of part to part. He draws out with relentless consistency *their full implications and consequences*.

The path of 'no-thing' up the mount, the summit of 'nothing' is the consequence of God being God, infinite mystery, and man being in relation to him who lies outside the range of his senses and rational mind. We are 'for' and 'to' and 'in' this infinite mystery. It defines our being. We are transcendent and nothing must be allowed to hinder the flight of transcendence to love that 'wears the mask of nothingness'. That God is hidden no one denies theoretically, yet how many stand in the truth of this fact? How many are prepared to live with the full implications of this hiddenness? This is precisely what John would have us do. 'Among all creatures, the highest and lowest, there is not one that remotely resembles God.'[1] Yet we naturally persist in confusing him with creatures, seeing him alongside them, as one of them in fact, albeit the mightiest and the greatest. 'God transcends the intellect and is inaccessible to it.'[2] How far-reaching the consequences of this truth! 'God himself is night to the soul in this life.'[3] And man, rational, finite man, is 'towards' this inaccessible one and can find fulfilment only in him. How does he go? How does he get there? This is what John tells us.

[1]*Ascent*, bk 2:8.
[2]*Living Flame*, st. 3.
[3]*Ascent*, bk 1:2.

6

John is enamoured of human transcendence. 'One single thought of man is greater than all the world; only God is worthy of it.'[1] We are made for the infinite and degrade ourselves if we opt for less.

> The whole creation compared with the infinite being of
> God is nothing.
> All the beauty of creation compared with His beauty is
> sheer ugliness;
> all its delicate loveliness
> merely repulsive.
> Compared with the goodness of God
> the goodness of the entire world
> is rather evil.
> All wisdom, all human understanding beside his
> is pure ignorance . . .
> and so it is with sweetness,
> pleasures, riches, glory, freedom.[2]

This is a hymn to human transcendence not a denigration of created reality. John's pathway up the mount could rightly be entitled, 'On becoming human'.

'How strait is the way that leads to life' (Matt. 7:14). This word of Jesus is crucial for John. His drawing is an illustration of it. Jesus himself is the way; he is the mystery of God accessible to us. He is also the archetype of human trancendence. John's teaching is based on Jesus crucified. Everything in it is to show us how to live as Jesus lived in total obedience to the Father's call. In Jesus we learn what man is, what God intends him to be. He never deflected from the 'upward call', never compromised with what would have detained him within the limits of 'the world'. He never stood for himself, never claimed self-sufficiency and independence. He saw himself always as an emptiness for receiving his Father. Jesus 'was made perfect', achieved the term of transcendence. In reaching the Father he took us with him; and this marvellous

[1]*Maxims.*
[2]*Ascent*, bk 2:6.

7

work of reconciliation was wrought, not when he was acting with power and performing miracles, but when he was brought utterly low – emptied out, annihilated.[1]

Jesus is the way; he enables us to take the way he is. He is the door, the only door through which we reach the Father. 'O would that I could get spiritual persons to understand', cries John, 'that the road to God . . . lies in denying ourselves in earnest within and without and undergoing sufferings with Christ, annihilating ourselves in all things.'[2]

[1]ibid. bk 2:7.
[2]ibid.

1

Putting John in Context

John himself warns us that the *Ascent* and *Dark Night* are not easily understood. He warns us not to isolate passages or think we grasp his thought correctly until we have read the whole work through, and that more than once. One part throws light on another; everything must be seen in context. His subject matter is difficult and his style does not help. We must constantly question, 'is he actually saying what he seems to be saying?' Can we detect personal situational factors which are moulding his thought and expression? Can we with any confidence separate the unassailable, unchanging principles from irrelevancies? Yes, I think we can.

The *Ascent* would have benefited by good editing. It reads not so much as a literary unit but as a compilation of material prepared and used for different purposes of instruction and direction. There are tedious redundancies, repetitions, a disproportion of emphases and misplacement of material which would not be tolerated in a well-planned book. These not only hinder clarity but at times positively mislead. How helpful it would have been, for instance, if we had been told when he is hammering away at the mortification of *all* desires that he is referring to *sinful* desires. We have to wait until Chapter 11 before we receive this reassuring information. But then he *has* warned us not to draw premature conclusions! To my mind the most enlightening explanation of what John is really talking about in Book 1 of the *Ascent* is found in Book 3 (Chapters 16–25). Repetitious as it is we are tempted to slide over passages which we think we have read before though in a slightly different form. We easily overlook a

9

sentence that radically changes the perspective. Overall, however, is John's absolute conviction of the truth of his teaching.

John was trained in scholasticism and understandably employs scholastic philosophy with its view of man and the world as his framework. This philosophy with its endless divisions and subdivisions is alien to our way of thinking. We seek to unify. How easily we get the impression of departmentalism in John and of a programme to be pursued systematically. You begin by learning to control your lower nature; then something called the 'dark night' will come upon you. When you have dealt successfully with this you emerge into another phase. Your task now is to mortify your spiritual faculties – intellect, memory and will. You must practise faith, hope and charity. *Then* something quite awful is likely to happen called the 'dark night of the spirit'. After that, if you manage to get so far, you can hope for good things. This is of course totally false as we hope to show.

Whatever the difficulties it creates for us there is no doubt that scholasticism for John proved a useful device for revealing every aspect of our self-centredness, for ruthlessly exposing our escape routes. Through it he can show us how each single bit of ourselves, so to speak, has to be purified and handed over to God. He leaves us without excuse.

An all-important question when we want to understand John is to ask for whom he is writing. Generally speaking he has in mind particular friars and nuns of Carmel, and more often nuns. John is frequently envisaged as a co-founder of the Discalced Carmelite Order, enjoying the same influence and prestige as St Teresa. This is not so. He was by no means a dominant figure in his lifetime and seems to have influenced or been known by relatively few members of the Order. He had very little to do with the actual shaping of affairs within the Reform. His influence was spiritual and appears to have been limited to certain convents and monasteries. Generally recognised as exemplary, he yet passed unnoticed. St Teresa had cause to complain that no one seemed to worry that John was held prisoner by the Calced in cruel conditions: 'Does no one remember that saint!' she exclaimed. And yet it is doubtful whether she herself recognised his full spiritual stature. Inevitably her opinions, bruited or tacit, would influence her daughters. There *are* times indeed when John reached out to a wider audience, but on the whole he was concerned with the friars and nuns he knew and women living very retired lives.

Now the Teresian Reform to which John belonged (indeed was the first male member) embodied a spirit that was wholly eremitical. The vocation of the Discalced Carmelite was to a withdrawn solitary life, which thereby demanded a strict limiting of the created means to God. It must be stressed here that this is not the normal vocation of the Christian people, it is a special one. We must bear in mind that most often John's counselling on solitariness, forgetfulness of creatures, avoidance of converse with others and unnecessary business is specifically directed to those whose special vocation demanded this retirement. What is right for people whose inherent calling is to be in the midst of the world would be an infidelity in those chosen to live apart and serve the Church in this particular way.

The earliest writing of John that we have, known as the *Cautions*, is one that often gives most offence and is a good illustration of the point made above. These *Cautions* were almost certainly written for the Carmelite nuns of Beas with whom he was very familiar; a young group in the main and at the beginning of their religious life. John as their spiritual director was intimate with each sister and with the community as a whole, and therefore in an excellent position to assess the quality of life within the enclosure. He had a thorough understanding of St Teresa's vision of Carmel. She had taken him to the foundation at Valladolid so that he would have first-hand experience of the new way of life before he embarked on it himself. As the enclosure was not yet erected John could associate with the sisters and to some extent share their community life. According to St Teresa he was given an exact knowledge of everything; the ascetical practices, how the time of recreation was spent together, the

11

warm friendly relations between the sisters and how Teresa had charged the prioress to be loving towards them – indeed she must strive to be loved so as to make obedience easy. All this is therefore taken for granted in the *Cautions*.

At the same time John knew that the heart of the Carmelite vocation is to live in solitude with God alone and community life is organised precisely to enable each one to do so. How easily a small enclosed, intellectually impoverished group of women could become trapped in the petty nothings of community life, nosing into one another's business, yielding to immature emotions or purely natural likings and attractions. What more harmful and disturbing in such a group than partialities, jealousies, lack of mutual trust, waste of time and talk of what is unimportant? John wants his sisters to use community life to the full, for the purpose it is ordained to help, and to avoid its inevitable risks and dangers.

It is against this background that we must interpret the chilling injunction that has estranged so many from John and made them accuse him of insensibility: 'Do not love one person more than another . . . love all equally and forget all equally be they relatives or not . . . Look upon all as strangers.' Harsh words indeed if taken at their face value! But do they in fact demand more than Jesus demanded? No one, however dear, must be allowed to distract us from perfect discipleship. We know he was not condemning love, affection, family devotion, but he wanted us to be free for loving God and our neighbour and thus grow to full personhood. This is John's aim too. The religious vocation calls for a leaving of family and home; it would be a sham indeed to live bodily inside the enclosure but emotionally and imaginatively outside. 'Live in the monastery as if you alone lived in it.' There is no question of an aloof uncaring association merely convenient for social or economic purposes; on the contrary John is pointing the way to a mature, healthy and ultimately wholly pure and Christlike love. He is warning against a wrong kind of involvement that not only distracts a religious from her purpose but damages love and deprives another of her privacy.

We must let others be, trust them implicitly, always presume on their good intentions whatever 'seems'. Inevitably there will be things that puzzle, perhaps scandalise us – if we let them. Do not allow your mind to run in and out of other people's lives, he counsels; do not scrutinise their actions or attempt to discover their motives. 'Judge not,' says Jesus – because you cannot. Trust, interior silence regarding others, furthers love. The opposite leads to evil.

It is significant that the women who received these 'harsh', 'inhuman' counsels had no inhibitions about telling John of their troubles, their loneliness, even that they felt hurt because he had not written and seemed to be forgetting them. Clearly they did not expect a stinging rebuke and a reiteration of forgetfulness: 'Forget me just as I forget you.' Rather they anticipated a sensitive consoling reply. The same man who wrote the *Cautions* penned the following to a laywoman penitent:

> Jesus abide in you. I thank him that he has given me his grace not to forget the poor, to drop them into oblivion as you say. I am furious at the idea that you really believe this; it would be too bad after all you had done for me when I least deserved it. To forget you would be the limit! How could I forget one who is in my very soul as you are?

He tells her that he has felt all her grief, emptiness and loneliness and is moved beyond what his pen can express. She must write more often and her letters must be longer. Instances like this should help us to a cautious, intelligent interpretation of John's 'world-denying' demands.

John as a person seems to have been singularly self-reliant from his earliest years, a man of great inner resources. It is doubtful if he ever knew a real emotional need for others. As against the large collection of St Teresa's letters we have only a handful of John's and it would be unwise to draw too many conclusions from their contents. Nevertheless it is noteworthy that there is nothing in them to compare with Teresa's naked exposure of human loneliness, her need for love and reassurance. In John's letters, gentle, sensitive, tender though they

13

are, he is always the master, guide and consoler; he himself remains secret. This great emotional strength – most clearly manifest in his endurance of nine months solitary confinement in appalling conditions of cold, heat, dirt, starvation, lack of light and air; subject to cruel handling and brainwashing, with absolutely nothing to occupy his time – was no doubt the fruit of his deep spirituality, but we can assume a fine, natural basis for this spiritual firmness.

It seems John was endowed with an exceptionally finely-honed serene temperament. There was never a time when he was not oriented towards God and striving to love him. By the time he was thirty-four or thirty-five he was an indubitable authority on spiritual matters which few attain whatever their age. St Teresa recognised his early maturity and his independence of thought and judgment. She admits that it quite annoyed her!

Now it could well be impossible for such a temperament, and one so highly disciplined, to analyse fully his own successful journey. Could he know what had constituted the essence of that journey and what were the relatively unimportant elements deriving from his own temperament and upbringing? He would perhaps see things in others he could not understand; much that to him seemed useless distraction, irrelevant to a total search for God, yet in reality perhaps *necessary for them*. Maybe he could not fully discern what was merely natural weakness and defect of temperament and, as such, no obstacle to union with God. This suggestion is put forward tentatively, but with some conviction that it will prove useful for interpreting John's teaching.

John was naturally drawn to solitude and for him it would be plain as day that, all things considered, solitude was *the* place for the rendezvous with God. Unlike Teresa he was not at home in the hustle and bustle of life. The countryside, lonely places full of music for his heart, these were his natural abode. No doubt it was his own experience to:

> suffer greatly in dealing with men and the affairs of the
> world, because these things hinder rather than help in the

search for the beloved . . . The keepers who go about the city are the affairs of the world which, when they 'find' someone seeking after God, inflict upon him much grief and loathing . . . Worldly affairs take away the cloak of peace and the quiet of loving contemplation.[1]

But what if our service of God demands dealing with worldly affairs, as is the case for most people? Is that to be deprived of contemplative graces? Of course not. How could it! God would be denying his own ordinances. Here in this lament of John's we hear the voiced pain of someone who both by vocation and temperament was called to solitude, writing to others called to a similar solitude. Kind, loving, concerned though he was, we cannot but feel he had little practical notion of what life was really like for the ordinary man and woman, of how the world turns and things get done.

John achieved holiness at an early age. Teresa met him when he was only twenty-six and bore witness to his maturity. He could disconcert her with his independence of mind. In all his writings we find the words of the master – authoritative, certain, serene. His way to holiness had been one of withdrawal, 'abstinence from joy and pleasure'. This suited him and had worked. But does it follow that such a withdrawal, such an abstinence is for everyone who would go the whole way to God?

We have looked at factors in John's way of writing which could lead to misrepresentation of his true mind. We have considered for whom he wrote; considered his own particular temperament. There is another very important consideration which he refers to in the Prologue to the *Ascent*: widespread ignorance regarding the true path to union with God.

As we have pointed out, most of his writing was for the guidance of Carmelite nuns. They, along with other women of that era, were kept in a state of ignorance and were entirely dependent on priests for instruction and guidance. But where were the competent guides? John has some harsh things to say about incompetent directors. They are presumptuous,

[1] *Canticle*, st. 9, n.

15

authoritarian, ignorant, 'blacksmiths', 'hewers of wood' who cause irreparable harm to those they direct; and this state of affairs, says John, is common.

Here is a man of rare wisdom, clear-sighted, closely united to God and knowing himself called to communicate to others the 'science of love'. All around are false notions, spurious spiritualities, paranormal experiences so abounding as to be almost normal, a craving for the sensational, sensual indulgence in the name of divine love. In other circles there was a reaction, a clamping down on any pretensions to mystical experience and advanced prayer; an insistence on external practices, harsh penances ('animal penance', John was to call it); discursive meditation held out as the proper and only safe mode of prayer. Such appalling ignorance and clumsiness in so sacred an area where successful direction could mean infinite gain and mistaken direction almost infinite loss!

John is determined to do what he can. He will not take any risks. As he cannot always do so personally he will direct his sisters and others through his writings. He will avoid all danger. His readers shall have the way spelled out for them starkly, in black and white with no greys. He will set them on a way that all but ensures safety. Follow this way, he is saying, and you will get to the end. It is as if someone has to send children on a long journey and may not accompany them himself. He gives them food and the strictest instructions to follow the path absolutely. They must not stop to satisfy their curiosity in this or that, a lark's nest, an empty cottage; no, they must go straight on. On no account may they eat berries or fruit from the trees but must be content with the food they carry. He knows well that in imposing these restrictions he is depriving the children of good things. There are lovely things to be seen which could enrich them, but there are dangers too – concealed animal traps, adder's nests. There are nourishing sustaining berries and herbs but poisonous ones also. The children lack the experience to know the difference and their only safety lies in being forbidden all. Were he to accompany them himself it would be different. He would show them how to select, how to enjoy and profit by all the good things in a way that would help them to journey more quickly and with greater gain. Without his personal presence the risks are too great; he must forbid everything.

Our position today is very different. We are educated and, if we are truly sincere in our desire for God, can discover how to use good things as helps towards him. We may go further. To deliberately cultivate a negative attitude to created things, to reject them on principle, would be a perversion and, far from ensuring a straight path to God could take us away from him. One of the Spirit's gifts to our times is a true appreciation of created values, an awareness that God is glorified in our use and enjoyment of all he has given.

2

Beginning the Ascent

The language of John's book, *The Ascent of Mount Carmel*, is abstract and arid; only rarely does it stir the heart. However not infrequently we find in the lyrical *Spiritual Canticle* or *Living Flame* the same thought expressed more appealingly. In the first stanza of the *Canticle* together with its commentary we are presented with a conversion experience. A person is awakened to reality, begins to understand something of what life is all about, begins to look for God and under the influence of grace decides to seek him in earnest.

> Where have you hidden yourself, O my beloved?
> You leave me in my groanings.
> Shy as the deer you have fled away
> Leaving me wounded:
> I ran after you crying, but you were gone!

Are we likely to think when we know almost nothing of God, have only just turned to him, that we can make such a poignant exclamation our own? Is it fitting? Yes. John would have us understand that it is wholly fitting. Can I in truth call God my beloved? Can I truly say I am wounded with love of him? Yes, John says, you most assuredly can. The time will come, if we are faithful, when these words will have infinitely more reality for us, but even now in the beginning they are true.

The human heart, John shows us here, has a beloved, its first and only love, and he is the object of its desire. We are seeking him in all our seekings even when we betray him, substituting for him the myriad beauties of creation which he has set on our path to point us to him and kindle desire. We bear within our very substance an open wound of longing, dissatisfaction. We experience this but most often do not recognise its cause. We seek to assuage our wound in one way or another but there is no healing of it apart from him. It is a blessed thing to suffer from this wound and the greater the pain the greater the blessedness. John will develop this idea later:

> O you who were created for union of love with God himself and whom he is ever attracting to himself, what are you doing with your precious lives, with your time? You are labouring for nothingness and all you think you possess is pure misery. O terrible human blindness. So great a light about you and you do not see it! So clear a voice sounding and you do not hear![1]

Each of us by the very fact of being human is made for union with God. It is our nature to be thus. We have within ourselves, or rather we *are* ourselves, a potentiality for this union. This potentiality however will not develop automatically; we must choose to develop it and allow God to develop it. John can at times give the impression that something has to be added to our nature for union with God, distinguishing as he does between the natural and the supernatural. But in the *Canticle* he makes it clear that God dwells within us *as human beings*. God is within, offering himself to be known and loved. We must wake up and seek him where he is, that is, within ourselves.

> O most beautiful of creatures, transcendent spirit, who long to know where your beloved is and where you may find him so as to be united with him. He dwells within you. You are yourself the tabernacle, his secret hiding place. Rejoice, exult, for all you could possibly desire, all your heart's longing is so close, so intimate as to be within you; you cannot *be* without him.[2]

[1] *Canticle*, st. 39.
[2] ibid. st. 1.

To say God is within us is to say we are transcendent, for-God, our being subsisting in him and for him. He is our centre, our term, our completion. Later on John is going to speak of something new, what he calls infused or mystical contemplation. This is a divine impetus, vivifying, energising, bringing into realisation what is *already there* as at the call of spring the seed begins to germinate. This is scriptural teaching. We must be born again of the Spirit. Without Spirit we remain flesh which cannot know God. The evolution of the butterfly is a marvellous image of what is meant here. The caterpillar must be 'born again'; it must receive an impetus to enable it to be transformed into a butterfly. But it has within it, in its caterpillar state, all the potential for this. Nothing new is added, what is already there is developed. So it is with us. God is our beloved in truth now, but will be so even more truly when we can call him that after long and generous effort and correspondence with his action. Then we are no longer our own but his! We are wounded with longing even now; what when we are one living wound, wide, deep, able to receive him fully! The spring of living water is within us, yet the mouth of it is so cluttered over that we cannot perceive its scent or hear its murmur. Clear away the rubbish, cries John, and the spring will leap forth to be 'joined to what it belongs to' – the sea. He teaches us how to clear away the clutter we do not even recognise as such.

John of the Cross is the evangelist of the hiddenness of God: 'God is night to the soul in this life.' Rigorously he would detach us from any desire to experience him with our ordinary equipment of sense – yet how insidiously we yearn to do so! We should never be satisfied with these counterfeits. Deeper than our desire for clear knowledge, for 'experience', is the longing for what cannot be grasped or held. We do not really want mystery to be dissolved in clarity; we *do* want it close, intimate.

We ourselves are mystery and our proper ambience is mystery. When we speak of God's hiddenness we are saying he is the answer to our yearning. He is unfathomable mystery offered to us. Through Jesus he reveals himself not only as

20

our beloved – the object of desire – but as our lover. Then
we realise that he has always been our beloved for the simple
reason that he *is* our lover. We learn that there is a fulfilment
to our endless longing but not within ourselves, not within
the limitations of this world or our own achievements, but as
pure gift. There is an inevitable conflict between our true self
and its deepest desire to be enfolded, possessed by our
beloved, and the innate drive to control, possess, to find
fulfilment within ourselves, of ourselves. This we can call the
ego. It is our basic self-orientation which is a dead end. Let
us say the true self is loyal to transcendence, the ego betrays
it and settles for limitation. 'We must courageously resolve
to pass both interiorly and exteriorly beyond the limits of our
own nature, so as to enter illimitably within the supernatural
which has no measure and contains all measure within itself.'[1]
But it is *precisely* our nature to go beyond the limits of our
nature so as to enter into God! The self must triumph over
the ego.

Turning now to the *Ascent* we understand that John is not
demanding that we cast a pall over all created things and
live in some sort of void but that we impose a night on the
ego. 'It is not the things of this world that ensnare and injure
the soul, for they do not enter within it, but the desire for
them which abides within it, that is the ego which always
seeks itself and therefore abuses and destroys.'[2] The ego curls
inwards and, like a carnivorous flower, draws everything else
within it, destroying both them and itself. This ego-centred
movement is a perversion, it is disobedience in the fullest
sense. It is sin. In Paul's terms it is the flesh that lusteth
against the spirit. Called beyond ourselves to the enfolding
transforming love of the infinite, and never happy save in
obedience to this call, we nevertheless shrink from commitment to it. Innately obstinate in us (and how strong!) is
that which expects, demands, looks for fulfilment within this

[1]*Ascent*, bk 2:4.
[2]ibid. bk 1:3.

21

world, even though we know experientially and intellectually that it cannot be.

The New Testament speaks eloquently under different images of this perverse movement of the human spirit, this fundamental disobedience, this desire to be 'god'. It takes various forms, from crude materialism, 'their gods are their bellies', to high spiritual pretensions; be it fervent keeping of the law and moral righteousness, or the denial of matter in favour of a 'purely spiritual' religion of gnosticism. This is the 'aeon' over which Satan rules (Eph. 2:2), the world which is the enemy of God. It is not the world of visible reality, God's beautiful creation which he finds 'so good', but a realm of being that chooses to be subject to its own will alone. It chooses to settle within its own limited frontiers and thus be its own satisfaction, its own god. It is a denial of transcendence, a refusal to recognise fundamental, total dependence on God. Paul is only too aware of how all of us are caught in the meshes of this unholy web; it is an atmosphere we breathe from the moment we are born. It is a slavery though we know it not. 'Who can deliver us?' cries Paul, and he answers with the triumphant cry of 'Jesus'. What can overcome the 'world', the world that is the enemy of God? Faith – faith that acclaims Jesus as the Son of God.

We have to lose sight of the ego, put it in the 'night', outside the range of our vision. We have to make up our minds to want God alone whatever the cost: 'The will ought to rejoice in nothing but in that which is for the honour and glory of God.' From the depths of our being, with all the sincerity and determination we have, we must explicitly and continually affirm that we hand ourselves over to God, that we are not concerned with ourselves, we want nothing for ourselves. This is to put our selfishness in the night, what John calls the active night, and in Book 1, our present concern, the active night of sense. In Books 2 and 3 he will speak of the active night of spirit, true to his logical scholastic division of man into sensual and spiritual.

The *Ascent* teaches what *we* must do to impose night on the ego, but it is incomplete without its sequel, the *Dark Night*, which tells us what *God* does and how we respond to him. These different nights are separated only logically. This is John's way of demonstrating how profound, how searching and absolute our purification must be: a purification which is a *becoming*, a taking over of non-being by being, a becoming which is coexistent with our union with God.

Steeped in the vision of truth of what is God and what is anti-god: 'flesh', 'world', 'idol'; John of the Cross sets out in his own unique way to show us practically, in our daily existence, in all the reality of our human complexity, how to live 'faith' which alone sets us free. Faith is perfect obedience, perfect response to the call of love, loyalty to our transcendence. Faith can only develop in so far as we impose 'night' on the 'lust of the flesh', that ego-desire to be for oneself, to have for oneself, to control, to possess, to be self-centred instead of God-and-other centred. He will show us how to believe in Jesus, how to fix our gaze on the 'spotless mirror of the eternal Father'.

It is easy to say we want God, that we hand ourselves over to him. John reveals that we scarcely know what we are talking about. He exposes our deepest selfishness and shows us just what true spirituality really is. Perhaps no one save Thérèse of Lisieux has equalled him in this. Only progressively, and that under the influence of the passive night, do we begin to get a glimpse of the extent of our self-seeking.

Ego-desire must be conquered by another and greater desire, 'love and imitate Jesus Christ who in his life had and sought no other satisfaction than that of pleasing his Father'.[1]

> My hearts knows you now
> Jesus Christ my Lord
> and everything worldly
> has lost its meaning. (Phil. 3:8)

The appetite for self-gratification must be replaced with an appetite for Christ, for living our human lives as he lived his. Everything has to be seen and judged in the light of Jesus'

[1]ibid. bk 1:13.

23

teaching. The love of Jesus Christ must become our one motivating force.

We come to know Jesus and how he lived by meditation. Two activities dominate the nighting of the ego – meditation and asceticism. The word 'meditation' has become a sort of code word with John.

While retaining its specific meaning it serves as a useful shorthand for *all our own efforts* to advance, and this includes asceticism. Our own efforts can never of themselves achieve the essential nighting of the ego, only God can do this; but we have to work hard to make it possible for him to do so. No one will insist more than John that the mountain cannot be scaled by ourselves. Nevertheless he is equally emphatic that unless we do undertake a thorough asceticism we cannot even begin the ascent. This stage of great human effort with what we may here call 'ordinary grace' cannot be skipped.

John does not mention giving time to prayer. This, together with reception of the sacraments, is taken for granted. He was addressing people for whom both were essential features of daily life. To set aside a time for prayer each day is in itself an asceticism. Unless we are prepared to do this unfailingly day in, day out, whatever the pressures, there is little point in taking John as guide. He does not spend time instructing us in the early practice of prayer for he knows this stage is well catered for and is anxious to push on into his own special field.

Certainly methods of prayer will differ according to temperaments and abilities, in the early stages and throughout our whole life, but what is of the utmost importance is persistent pondering on the Scriptures. The New Testament must be the basis of our intellectual knowledge of God and his will for us. Only thus can we rightly interpret every other form of revelation. Our 'appetite' for Jesus must be sharp and unabating. 'Those who truly love God are no laggards in their efforts to find him, and when they have done all they can still they are not satisfied, thinking they have done nothing.'[1] 'Tell me, has he passed by you?' the seeker

---

[1] *Canticle*, st. 3.

asks of all creatures. The whole of life has to do with the beloved; he is to be found everywhere, in everyone and everything. We question everything by reflection and action. Thinking must of necessity play a vital role, and how essential it is to think rightly of God and his creation. Jesus Christ is our key. Today we have unparalleled opportunity of knowing him, his mind, his values, of viewing God and the world with his vision. Modern scholars have opened up the Scriptures for us as never before. We must avail ourselves of their labours, must enter in and make them our own.

Everything we learn about Jesus must then be translated into living. John's ascetic instructions as well as all else in his teaching are a way of translating into action the fundamental truth of Jesus – that he lived for his Father's will and that this will was his sole satisfaction. It is easy enough to imagine that we do God's will, that we love him, when we have but a little light. John was a man who really did know him, really did love him and lived by his light. He shows us something of what it means to live for God, to hand oneself over to him completely. As already pointed put, and it must be repeated often, we cannot bring *ourselves* to complete surrender, God must achieve this for us; nevertheless whether he does or not depends on the realism of our desire.

When I think of a life wholly handed over to God, instinctively I turn to Thérèse of Lisieux. There have been others no doubt who similarly gave God their all, but of her growth in the Holy Spirit we have documentation. We are allowed to see her at it day after day. Hers was a wholehearted determination to give him everything and she saw life only in terms of this self-donation. She could express it so simply at the end of her life; 'I ignored myself and sought myself in nothing.' What does this mean in practice? Have we any idea how encompassing it must be? John, with his usual relentless analysis, helps us to discover the answer.

3

The Denial of Desire

The early chapters of Book 1 of the *Ascent* treat of the whys and wherefores of self-denial. They speak of the evils of immortified 'desire', the need for the 'night' and the benefits that flow from it. Chapter 13 then gives us a programme of asceticism for surely and swiftly entering into this night.

We shall consider John's instructions at considerable length for two reasons. First because they are so much 'John' – all-embracing, absolute to the point of offence, and secondly to dispel the offence. On the one hand we must never whittle down his demands with their implicit 'unless you answer them you can never reach full union with God'. On the other hand we must make sure that we *do* understand what he is asking and see that anything less must of necessity mean a clinging to self instead of surrendering the whole of ourselves to God.

The different sets of maxims cover various aspects of our activity and response to life. The first set deals with our senses and the principle of pleasure and at first glance we might draw a sharp breath. But note the exact wording: 'Every satisfaction offered to the senses *which is not for the honour and glory of God* must be renounced and rejected for the love of Jesus Christ . . . That *which tends not to the service of God* . . . those things *which do not lead you nearer to God.*' Now do we not implicitly imagine that there are some activities that are obviously pleasing to God, those we consciously and specifically do for him? On the whole we are ready to assume that these will be costly. Then there are other things we know are sinful and should be avoided. But then there are a vast multitude of activities – in fact those which fill most of our lives – that really have nothing to do with him, are in fact neutral. Is this not our working assumption? Yet if we gave thought to the matter we would see this conclusion as completely false. John is expressly saying that there is *no* neutrality; an action is for the honour and glory of God and leads us to him or else it is sinful.

It is God's plan for us that everything should lead us to him, everything be a revelation of him. Creatures are an essential means to God; he comes to us through them, and in the early stages *only* through them. To receive him thus is to worship him, whereas conscious advertence to him all the time would be impossible. Every proper use we make of creation is for his glory because it aids our growth and development and helps us towards becoming mature and loving persons.

John can sometimes give the impression that we must renounce all love of creatures: 'He who loves anything besides God is incapable of divine union.'[1] What chilled me in former days was the thought that somehow I had to be satisfied with naked God; I had to live in a void in which only God was and be satisfied with him alone. Well, I was not and could not be for I could not conceive of him in any way. I knew I *needed* creatures. But of course God is not the supreme object among many objects, so that if you love these other objects you are loving him less – as though love of people and things rivals love for God! God is not an object and therefore lies totally outside the range of our thinking, imagining, loving. One of the implications of his hiddenness is that he cannot be held, looked at, enjoyed directly in this life. He is in all; things *are* only because of his self-communication to them. To love anyone or anything purely is to love him; to relate to them in accordance with his designs is to be in union with him. In our unsullied enjoyment of creatures, in our delight in others, we are enjoying and delighting in him. We ask everyone and everything about him: 'Has he passed by you?

[1]*Ascent*, bk 1:4.

Show me what he is like. Tell me of him.' We ask these questions not merely with the mind in meditation; we ask in action by using creatures as they should be used.

However it is not natural to us to treat everything properly. We have to labour for purity of vision, hearing, touching, tasting, smelling. Sedulously we must avoid every act that is sinful (that is, selfish). Everything we perceive that does not help us to grow in love of God and others must be denied at whatever cost. 'If your eye is a cause of stumbling to you,' says Jesus, 'put it out.' A highly charged metaphor to impress on us the unutterable importance of pleasing God, living as he would have us live. Nothing counts beside this, not our pleasure and satisfaction, not an easy comfortable life, not wide experience of sense, not 'happiness' – *nothing*. All occasions of sin must be avoided absolutely in so far as depends on us. When they cannot be avoided and we find ourselves caught up in pleasures that do not help us to God then we must detach ourselves from them, refuse to savour them. But the pleasure that attends all innocent use of created things is to be enjoyed reverently and gratefully. There is no question of our denying ourselves just for the sake of doing so, as though this is what God wants. Why would he have attached pleasure to our natural functions if he saw it was best for us not to have it?

We need pleasure, but it may be that earnest love sees that we cannot hope to deny ourselves wrong pleasures unless we have undergone a preparatory discipline and learned to say no to perfectly innocent ones. This renunciation is for a purpose; one might say it is a temporary expediency. Our use of creatures, whether we forgo this or that, will be a very personal matter. Nobody can make rules for another. Needless to say we will need wise counsel for we are not good judges of our own motives. Our Lord wills us to seek light and guidance. But when all is said and done it is we who must make the decision, and never are we more lonely than when we do so in moral areas. Each has his or her own vocation in life with its own specific demands. No one can live out the full range of human/christian values. We have to choose, and the choice depends on the vocation to which God has called us. It is in the concrete circumstances of our lives that our imitation of Jesus takes place for he sought no satisfaction save his Father's good pleasure. It is he who gives us our vocation, invites us to do this or that. We may not decide to thrust on him what he does not want from us. He may call us to many pleasures in the things of sense or on the contrary lead us along an austere path.

There is always a danger for some devout people, perhaps ourselves among them, of wanting to snap tensions which we find unbearable; we do this by choosing a way of negation. It is as if we find life on the mainland just too occupying, distracting, defiling, and hie off to a desert island where we can be free of these disturbing elements. Forthwith we feel disencumbered, innocent as children with nothing save natural beauty assailing the senses. Yet we have cut ourselves off from real life and growth. Our ego is still in command no matter how pure and undefiled we may feel. Even when God summons some into a monastic enclosure how important it is that within the enclosure there be everything necessary for full human development, all those elements that lead to self-knowledge and purification. This was St Teresa's aim in organising her Carmel with its fine blending of eremiticism and community life. This was the environment with which John of the Cross was familiar. There will always be those however who, not really knowing God, will remain insecure, scrupulous and persistent in giving God what he is not asking. They will deny themselves intellectual and emotional stimulus, cutting off absolutely the 'non-sacral' – much easier and safer to cut off everything! What we have to do is to carefully distinguush between frivolous unthinking, purpose-less diversions (perhaps of a dubious nature) and those things which, with their attendant delight, foster our human growth. There is no easy way of knowing. It demands constant attention, with never the security of feeling we have got it just right, that we are mortified, we are giving him everything. It must not be a comfortable self-image we seek but God.

Perhaps the love and service of our neighbour above all

will be what in practice makes the choice for us of whether we take or renounce this or that. We are called to freedom in relation to all the things of this world, says Paul, but we must not abuse this freedom by indulging selfishness, rather we must become slaves of our brethren (cf. Gal. 5:13). The good of our neighbour must at all times come before our immediate satisfaction. How many, how constant, how unobserved even to ourselves will be the renunciations imposed on us by loving concern for others.

Far, far better than any deliberate programme of self-denial, which after all keeps us occupied with self, is a programme of love which seeks to please God in everything, seeks to serve our neighbour. Yet who can pretend the agenda is clear-cut? Who can cry at the end, 'I have completed it, not an item omitted'? There are obligations which stand out a mile and people of goodwill are not likely to ignore these, but what of the ambiguous situations? After all the needs of the neighbour are limitless; there is always something more to do, someone more to help. Do I forgo all recreations, all time 'for myself'? Do I give up all my possessions? Do I go down among the poor and live with them? Once again it is not we who take the initiative but God who invites. We must keep our eyes on him, our ear to the ground to catch his voice. We *shall* be shown, though we may not clearly perceive that we have been shown and may feel anything but pleased with ourselves, especially when we have taken what seems to be the easiest course, conceding to our own needs.

James and John approach Jesus somewhat brazenly: 'We want you to do for us whatever we ask of you.' Jesus counters pertinently, 'What do you want me to do for you?' They state their grandiose request: 'Grant us to sit, one at your right hand and one at your left in your glory.' We too want to 'share his glory', we want to know we have fulfilled our obligations to the last iota. A little further down the page of Mark 10 we get Jesus asking someone else, forcing him to look at his real intent: 'What do you want me to do for you?' How often we think we are asking God for godly things when in reality we are asking for self-inflation. This man makes a request that will always be answered when it is really meant: 'Give me sight.' Is there a more vital prayer? Ah, how rarely is it meant when uttered! To see is no easy matter. Later we shall have John drawing out the implications of 'receive your sight'.

It can be useful when studying this area of asceticism to read Chapters 16–24 of the *Ascent*. Much of the same ground is covered under what John calls the purification of the will. Likewise we do well to look at a small corpus of writing which, in my opinion, deserves far more attention than it receives; the *Cautions* and *Counsels to a Religious*.

Both of these latter works are directed specifically to Carmelites, the first most probably to nuns, the second certainly to a friar. Both deal with vital aspects of asceticism which are of universal relevance and are a more detailed version of the instructions in Chapter 13 of the *Ascent*. In the *Ascent* we have principles, directives; in the *Cautions* and *Counsels* we see them applied in the concrete. As with all John's teaching we are shown how, in practice, to live solely for God in evangelical perfection, and this is the calling of all Christians.

John is 'at home' in religious life, on familiar ground, moving at ease, handling his material with conviction and authority, whereas when he attempts to carry his principles into secular life we feel he is floundering. As we read through his treatment of detachment from joy in the use of temporal, natural, sensible goods (his own categories) we cannot avoid the impression that here is a man ill-at-ease in the workaday world. For him it is infinitely preferable to get rid of all possessions, remain celibate, live in retirement and give oneself up to prayer; all else is second best. John is a typical product of the devout of his times with their suspicion of the secular. We have come a long way since then. We have no fear of the secular for this is where God is. The whole world is the Lord's, he is in all and not only in one tiny consecrated corner. *All* is sacred, the house of the Lord and the gate of heaven. John might prefer everyone to be within the cloister but God does not!

All John writes must therefore be interpreted using the insights of our own day, but his basic principles remain unchallenged – nothing and no one can be our ultimate joy or security. There has to be detachment coupled with great involvement and one does not rule out the other. Take John's rather down-graded view of marriage, for example, and put it against our own developing appreciation of just what marriage is meant to be. It is *the* way *par excellence* for the vast majority to grow into freedom and fulness of love, the vehicle of transcendence. What discipline, sacrifice, asceticism will be needed for it to reach this ideal! And when the partners have truly become two in one and then comes the separation of death – how incalculable the wound! Yes, but the very fact that the marriage has reached fulfilment will mean that the other can stand alone, continuing to embrace life, growing in freedom and love. All human situations are open to God. Prayer, constant reflection on the gospel, desire, vigilance – these will reveal how, in the concrete, hour by hour, we find him in them, respond to him in them.

In Books 1 and 3 of the *Ascent* John gives instructions on how to calm the four natural passions of joy, hope, fear and grief. These passions together with the senses belong, according to scholastic psychology, to our lower nature. What is meant by them? I think if we considered the matter carefully we would see that our spontaneous primitive desire is for 'happiness'. We want to feel 'well', at ease in the world, contented, secure. This state can be summed up as a sense of wellbeing. It is what John means by the word joy.

We have an instinctual drive towards seeking a sense of wellbeing in whatever way we conceive of it. Unchecked by reason it is likely to lead us to immediate satisfactions of one kind or another. Hope is a similar drive which puts us in motion towards the attainment of our desired objective; we feel it is there to be had, that we have a right to it. When our wellbeing is threatened we are afraid; we dread feeling 'unwell', unhappy, insecure, miserable, unattractive, downcast. We fear all that is inimical to what we conceive of as our happiness. When we lack the sense of wellbeing we grieve.

32

But our true happiness lies in God and all our energy must be poured into surrendering to his will, not dissipated on things which will eventually pall. We must learn to make God our only joy and satisfaction, fearing only to miss him, to disappoint him; sad only for his grief. This will not come easily, it must be struggled for.

So powerful is our instinct for ego-satisfaction that John gives it no quarter. He advises a frontal attack. He wants us to go clean against our desire for satisfaction, pleasure, consolation and *seek* the opposites. Far be it from me to say such a course is unwise but at least I would warn of dangers and suggest that, for most of us, it is not the best way. For one thing, though its aim is to the contrary, such an approach tends to focus us on ourselves, there is something contrived and self-conscious in it. The more we can keep our attention off ourselves, forget ourselves, the better. Also it is another instance of snapping life-giving tensions. The healthiest, most effective way is to renew our fundamental intention of giving God everything, then fulfil our duties, serve our neighbour with all love regardless of whether it is pleasant or unpleasant to do so. Never fail to do a good work – thus John advises – because of lack of pleasure or sweetness; be ready to do those that are distasteful.[1] Only so can we become reliable and conquer our weakness. Even in spiritual exercises we must be indifferent and persevere whether they are pleasurable and satisfying or not.

The more we fix our hearts and minds on Jesus our Lord the less we shall notice whether things are hard or easy, whether we feel happy or sad. We must become unimportant to ourselves. When something happens and we feel hurt, angry, resentful, or when our longing for attention and love is aroused and then ignored or rebuffed by another we must just say: 'I am not interested, it is you I want.' Gradually the energy of emotion is transferred, its object changed. We are set free from self-centredness and we become people who *really* love, purely, selflessly, under stress and strain, not dependent

[1]see *Cautions*.

for our peace of mind on outward circumstances, able to cope with insecurity.

We cannot sufficiently stress the need for emotional control, especially today when the reaction to emotional repressions of the past has caused the pendulum to swing the other way. In certain circles feelings are taken as all-important. An enormous amount of attention is given to them with the result that people are very conscious of how they feel and quick to think they have an absolute right to feel 'well'. There is no question of saying that we should pay no attention to our emotions; they are signals telling us something about ourselves. We look to see what this 'something' is, but when we have discovered it, what then? Are we allowed any and every course of action to change our state of feeling? Sometimes discovering the cause of a strong emotion can change the emotion, dissipate anger, for instance, but this is not always so. It seems to me that sooner or later each of us has to learn to put up with painful emotions, pay little attention to them, get on with doing what we have to do, attending to our neigbours' welfare, putting all our trust in God. We who know Jesus can surely afford to feel insecure – if we do! We can afford to feel fragile, fearful. Surely these painful emotions can be an opportunity for pure trust.

Some natures suffer very much from inner turmoils, bouts of depression and resentment which they cannot will away. Ultimately there is nothing for it but acceptance, self-control, peace within turmoil. We must resolutely refuse to confuse these states of feeling which *feel* sinful with sin. Here John consoles us that though a person liable to these trials may imagine that the passion and turmoil darkens and defiles his soul, in reality it is not so. Contrariwise, in proportion to the resistance offered such a one gains strength, pureness, light, consolation and many other good things, for 'power is made perfect in weakness'.[1] Such afflictions are aptly linked with Paul's 'thorn in the flesh' and serve the same purpose in God's design. Surely then we can bring ourselves to accept

[1] *Ascent*, bk 1:12.

our difficult temperaments, our psychic wounds, our shadows which cause much pain and use them to grow in love, instead of wasting time and energy looking for the magic wand or the wizard who is to put it all right for us.

We find it hard to give up the idea that there is a magic answer somewhere, that it must be possible to get this burden off our backs. We have a deep conviction that we are being wronged: our environment is wrong, our companions are responsible; if we had a different job, if this person was not around, if, if, if. There is no answer but facing reality. Do we not see that the truly happy people are not those who have spent themselves avoiding life's difficulties, seeking escapes and alleviations, trying to control life so as to provide a secure base for the ego, but those who have done battle with themselves, who have tried, not to change the world but to change themselves, to adapt, to accept, to bend, to die. It is a strange thing that one of the hardest things some people are asked to do is precisely to stop being miserable, to choose to be happy in a world of limitations, the world that really is, not the world of make-believe! We prefer to cling on to self-pity, self-contempt, self-recrimination. At least it is safe. It means I cannot be disappointed and no one can blame me for not expecting too much of myself or of life. Such an attitude is an escape from living and loving. It is an egocentric prison.

We shall find John in the *Cautions* and *Counsels* setting us fair and square in the world of real people where our ego will get all sorts of knocks. Expect it, says John, want it. It is the means of purification and unselfing, yield yourself to it, do not hide away. Take a positive view of what seems negative. We are to be polished and fashioned by our fellow religious before we can be set in the building. How few of us are willing to see life and our associates in this light! John does not ask for great extraordinary things, but only for infinite care in all the details which go to make up daily life. We shall suffer from the temperaments and habits of others but they are workmen whose job it is to polish the stone before it can be fitted into the building. Some will chisel with words, others by what they do, others by what they think of us. All this is precious; want it, use it, do not shirk it. Of course this demands real faith which takes God with utter seriousness – our God, my God, always intent on bringing me to fulfilment in him. 'My Father is always at work' (John 5:17).

Our aim is certainly not freedom from emotion or such a levelling of emotion that we are never ruffled, never elated, never saddened, ceasing to respond vitally to things. What dull, half-persons we would be! We work to ensure that we are never governed by emotions, recognising that often our feelings do not tell us the truth about reality and then, gradually, by dint of constant effort our emotions will to a great extent behave themselves and function appropriately. We go on *liking* many things, having our natural preferences, but we *choose* to want only one thing – God's will. He becomes so much to us that is impossible for us to be profoundly moved by anything except in so far as he is concerned.

4

The Meaning of Freedom

The whole aim of John's asceticism is to release us from the tyranny of the ego. Influenced by his scholastic framework he seems to write as if the senses had a life of their own and must control their actions; that the appetites, passions and emotions must likewise curb themselves. But of course this is not so. It is really the *will*, the faculty of choosing, that is involved. True the eye sees, the ear hears automatically; passions are aroused automatically, but it is the will that must choose to turn away the eyes, refuse to listen, control the instincts. Everything therefore will depend on what I really want, what I prize, what I hold to be my true good. Meditation, as we have said, keeps us looking at the values of Jesus so that we may choose to make these our own. Jesus is always summoning us beyond ourselves to the Father, bidding us deny the powerful tendency to seek fulfilment within ourselves and the limits of the created, making the aggrandisement of the ego the implicit motivation of our thinking and acting.

A little honest reflection shows us that naturally we are our own horizon, the most important person in the universe. Our attention and energy are largely employed in looking after ourselves in one way or another. Education, culture, pressures of our social milieu impose a certain altruism but it is skin deep. All of us recognise some obligations to others, duties to be done, sacrifices to be made, but it largely lies within our own decision as to where we draw the line. We assume unquestionably that we have the right to be treated justly, allowed independence, be consulted, recognised, appreciated.

We are very, very important to ourselves and we demand that others recognise this importance. Of course often we do not get what we consider just treatment, adequate recognition, and this makes us angry and bitter. All sorts of devices will be employed even unconsiously to have our importance acknowledged. Often these devices are dishonest and unfair to our neighbour but we choose not to advert to the fact.

John says if you want God, if you want to begin the ascent of the mountain, then you have to make a decision against self-importance. You have to remove yourself from the centre-stage, see yourself as a member of a family, a community which you must serve. This is what Jesus taught and Paul after him. Never think yourself more important than others, never put yourself before them. John expresses it typically in hyperbolic language: do things which bring you into contempt and want others to do likewise. Speak disparagingly of yourself and contrive that others do so too. Think humbly and contemptuously of yourself and want others to do so as well. What odious creatures we should be were we to carry out these injunctions literally! Can we see what he is hinting at in the above? Instead of the words 'contemptuously', 'disparagingly', substitute 'little of'. Think little of yourself and be happy that others do not consider you very important. Have a lowly opinion of yourself, not in the sense of unhealthy self-denigration but in that you do not consider yourself the pivot of the universe. Keep correcting in the silence of your heart the contrary natural attitude. Keep reminding yourself that others are more important than you are, that their well-being is more than the satisfaction of your ego. Let your actions conform to this truth. Do not demand that circumstances change to fit you, do not labour to control events for your own benefit. See yourself as the servant of others.

Such a willingness to forget the ego, to lose sight of it, calls for firm faith in God's love. Each of us is utterly important to God; we can afford to relax a bit and let him look after our little selves. We tend to think that unless we take care of 'number one' nobody will. Faith tells us there is one who never takes his eyes off us, so much so that not a hair of our head is lost.

An obsession with self-importance enslaves us to human respect. Human respect means allowing the opinion of others to matter more than God's. It means more that we stand well in the world of human beings than before God. This enslavement must be broken. We have to fix our eyes on our Lord and do what we know to be right. We are what we are in his sight and what others think of us changes that not one iota. We are entangled in so many useless occupations, says John, trying to please ourselves and others, speaking, thinking, doing things that are useless and omitting others that we should do. We play to someone else's tune with flattery and compliments, we aim at being well thought of, giving pleasure, wasting so much of our energy and time.[1] Giving pleasure to others is not reprehensible – far from it – but to do so in order to be liked, favoured, to have our ambitions fulfilled or avoid censure? That is another matter.

It must be said that some persons by temperament are much more concerned than others with human respect. The advantage of this is that they quickly become aware of their weakness and are able to confront it. Others of a more independent inward nature seem to care little what others think, but they must watch. Virtue is never there from the start. They must work to acquire true freedom and humility. It may be that they are indifferent on many fronts but there are sure to be instances where they are deeply concerned to be thought well of and resent criticism. Again the emotionally insecure have to struggle hard for freedom, but often a purer, stronger virtue is the result. However the last thing any of us must aim at is a Miller of Dee attitude; 'I care for nobody, no not I!'

John considers that there are very few spiritual persons who arrive at perfect courage and resolution in their conduct, free of all human respect. Some try to be detached and think they are but they never entirely forget themselves on certain

[1]See *Canticle*, st. 28.

points regarding self-esteem and what the world thinks of
them. They never wholly despise appearances. They can
never say with the true bride: 'Being deeply in love I lost
sight of myself; and yet was found . . . They who truly love
make shipwreck of themselves . . .'[1]

This making ourselves of little account in a practical way
will greatly affect our relationships with others. We have
already drawn attention to the *Cautions* and *Counsels* on the
role others have in our purification. We can recall the same
again. Nothing so reduces the ego as the realities of living
with others and not demanding that they change so as to suit
ourselves. John is speaking of the religious life but surely his
words are relevant for every situation where men and women
rub shoulders together. God brings people into community
precisely in order to purify them as gold is purified with fire
and hammer. It is wholly to be expected that there are plenty
of trials and temptations, the fire of troubles and afflictions.
We must strive to bear them patiently as is God's will. 'Many,
not realising that they have entered religious life for this very
purpose endure others reluctantly.'[2]

What an enormous difference attitudes make. We shall
have to bear many difficulties from other people anyway. To
see in all these things God's will for our ascent to him and
to make up our minds to adopt a positive attitude makes
everything so much easier! John's asceticism taken at one
swallow can seem just too much, but lived out it can only be
happiness-giving. We are our own misery and affliction. Get
rid of the ego and we are truly happy and at peace.

To think little of ourselves, to see ourselves as servants,
means we are not likely to be interested in our neighbours'
frailties in order to sit in judgment. If we want something for
self, if we want to be a fine sort of person then we get a
strange satisfaction in seeing our neighbour faulty – it makes
us feel not so bad, perhaps even superior. Even very good
people can get some satisfaction out of gossip, especially that

[1] ibid. st. 29.
[2] See *Counsels*.

with a spice of scandal. John would have his religious live in the monastery as if each one were alone there and never meddle either in thought or word with what is happening around them. They must not discuss even interiorly the character, manner of life or business of their companions, nor must they ever be shocked. 'If we lived among angels some things would seem to be wrong to us because we do not understand.' What does he mean? Certainly he is not counselling us against a loving concern for others, an awareness of their needs, or against real involvement with our neighbour. He is counselling us against all that comes under the heading of gossip whether interior or exterior. Our neighbour's character, affairs, behaviour are not proper subjects for our diversion and amusement. People who want to live for God must not entertain themselves maliciously with the lives of others. It shows a lack of respect and love. Such inner, let alone articulated, gossip is never without some malice and it derives from wanting the exaltation of our own ego.

What John has to say on obedience in the *Cautions* and *Counsels* may also at first sight seem to have little to do with secular life, but as always we must search for the underlying principle behind his instructions. What is involved is true humility, that refusal to make ourselves the centre of the world. Obedience in the gospel sense is essentially obedience to the Father as his will is manifested to us. It is obedience to our transcendent destiny. To be disobedient is to refuse our destiny, to decide for ourselves what is for our good, how our lives should be arranged, what we have a right to. It is an expression of non-faith and an assertion of the ego. Obedience cuts right across this. If we would be utterly obedient to the 'upward call' then we must learn how to submit ourselves to others, to circumstances, to the community welfare. Our will, our choice, must be in a very real sense to be without choice, waiting on God, abandoned, prepared to let this or that go, to be redirected, have our plans upset and so forth. It does not imply complete passivity, lack of initiative; it does mean flexibility, detachment, flowing from the faith-filled vision that discerns 'it is the Lord' – the Lord revealed not directly but through other human beings and events.

The stress on unimportance in no way overlooks the God-given need within each of us to be loved and accepted. It is surely *God's* will that his children meet with such always, finding in this a reflection of his own love and acceptance. In so far as it depends on us we must give these to all we encounter. However the fact remains that we are limited, fallible, sinful, blind, and so often we suffer from one another, feeling we are overlooked, undervalued. We must be prepared to be so and maintain peace of heart. We cannot accept and love others completely until we are free of our ego and it is the weaknesses, limitations, even downright malice of others that, if we but accept, exorcises this tyrant.

In his writings John often speaks of refreshment of spirit, how freedom from the ego brings peace. Indulging our selfishness only wearies us. The ego is like a child, fractious, restless, wanting now this, now that, never content with what is given.[1] Afflictions and pain flow from the ego, refreshment from the Spirit of God. The two cannot dwell together. We all know what it is to be tormented and afflicted, labouring under a burden of anxiety and desire. 'Cast it aside by coming to me,' says Jesus. 'I will refresh you.'[2] As fog darkens the sky and obscures the sun, or as a dirty mirror distorts an image, so the unbridled ego blocks light. Our natural power of reasoning is affected; we cannot see things as they are, cannot evaluate objectively while dominated by emotion and selfish desires. Still more, we are prevented from receiving the infused divine light. The finest intellect in the world cannot perceive truth while the heart is under the sway of selfishness.[3]

What does it mean for the soul to be defiled, polluted? Our nature is to be all aspiration, a leaping upwards towards fulness of life in God; it is to be a purity able to reflect the beauty of God, an emptiness to receive plenitude – 'O most beautiful of creatures!' By going against that true nature

[1] cf. *Ascent*, bk 1:6.
[2] ibid. bk 1:7.
[3] ibid. bk 1:9.

(which is what we do when we allow the ego to dominate us) we corrupt it. The fouling of pure water, the putrification of matter are weak images for this corruption. It is those who are very close to God who really see this, who are appalled at what sin does to a human being, for they see what a human being is meant to be.[1]

We have one dynamism of choice. That dynamism must be controlled, concentrated, otherwise it ceases to be dynamic and is like a worn out battery driving nothing. If we do not know what we really want, if we vacillate, allowing ourselves to be drawn hither and thither, we become enfeebled and our faculty of choice is weakened. We must decide what we really want and concentrate on that. 'The soul whose will is torn between trifles is like water which never rises because it is running through an outlet down below.'[2]

'I keep my strength for you', is a favourite idea of John's. The way to grow in love for God, to strengthen motivation, is precisely to keep the will directed, to bring it back when it has strayed. This fidelity opens us to divine influence without which little can be achieved.

John then voices a question which he presumes his reader is asking. Must every desire be quenched before we can be united with God or is it enough to have denied those of greater moment? After all it is an enormous thing to expect that we be free from every attachment. He replies with simple logic. Union with God means precisely *union*; if we choose something contrary to what God chooses for us then we cannot be in union with him. If we look at the path up the mountain and then at the paths to left and right we shall see what he means. The side paths represent diversions, a turning away from God in greater or lesser degree. You cannot go straight up the mountain and at the same time take a diversion. Here John falls back on the classical division of sin into mortal sin, venial sin and imperfections, yet he supersedes this view. He expresses it thus:

[1]ibid. bk 1:9.
[2]ibid. bk 1:10.

43

We must not, deliberately and knowingly
assent with the will to any imperfection,
and we must have such self-control and freedom
as to be able to reject every such desire
the moment we are aware of it . . .
I say 'knowingly'
for without deliberation and a clear perception
of what we are doing,
or because it is not wholly in our power,
we may easily give way to imperfections and venial sins
and natural desires.
It is of such sins as these, not entirely voluntary,
that it is written
'A just man shall fall seven times and rise again.'
But a voluntary, deliberate choice,
however slight the object,
prevents not only union
but all progress.[1]

John here is making a very important point. Sin is in the will.
It is a 'no' to the will of God, and the occasion of this can,
objectively, be small. It is the *deliberate* choice not to give God
what he is asking. We must not be hoodwinked by the
apparent slightness of the 'matter' as we would say in the old
days. What counts, what is grave, is a fully deliberate no with
our eyes wide open. How could we think that this and loving
God are compatible? The occasions can be insignificant –
John lists a few: we prefer a particular person's company to
what we know is God's will at a given moment. We know
that association with such or such a one interferes with our
duties, draws us away from the love and service of God but
we choose not to break with them. A religious likes a
particular cell and makes a fuss when asked to change,
wangles it so he can remain where he is; or he is demanding
and fastidious over food; indulges in tittle-tattle and gossip.
In themselves these are not crimes but they show clearly that
we are not set on giving God everything. We want lots of

[1]ibid. bk 1:11.

little gratifications which, at given times and circumstances, do not accord with God's will for us and are not our true good.

Good people have to be very honest with themselves. They are not likely to commit sins involving grave matter but unless they have resolutely set their hearts on God they may well be less careful in other areas. For instance they are not likely to wrong their neighbour in a big way, such as fraud. But what about his reputation? No, not gross calumny, just little insinuations, pregnant silences? Committed knowingly these are every bit as serious and as real a 'no' to God as flagrant injustices.

The most destructive 'no' is that involving full knowledge and consent. But we can be saying no to wanting to know; we do not want to see that such and such a practice or habit is contrary to God's will. This is a prolonged 'half-no'. If we wanted we could pull it into the light and see it for what it is but we would rather leave it in shadow.

There is of course a blindness inherent in the human condition; we are born blind and must wait for the Lord to give us sight. Growth in spirituality is synonymous with growth in sight. At times we can indeed 'see' yet be too weak to integrate in actual living what we understand intellectually. Provided we go on trying, these things in no way prevent God's work in us. They convince us rather of our poverty and need of him. What matters is the resolute *will* to give God here and now what he is asking. That is all we can do and all that matters. Let us do this and we shall grow in understanding and love. We are strengthened and enlightened by every choice of God's will, weakened and blinded to some extent by every refusal.

John closes the first book of the *Ascent* with twelve epigrammatic injunctions which, he says, are directed not to bringing us to the foot of the mountain but to its summit, 'the high estate of union with God'. They apply preeminently to what is spiritual and interior but nevertheless have relevance for the sensible and exterior. It is as if he cannot wait to arrive

at his chosen subject. He is all eagerness to introduce us to
the mysterious ascent of the mount – the passive night.

> That you may have pleasure in everything, seek pleasure
> in nothing.
> That you may know everything, seek to know nothing.
> That you may possess all things, seek to possess nothing.
> That you may be everything, seek to be nothing.

Pleasure, knowledge, possessions, fulness, these comprise the
object of all our desire and striving. We are meant to have
them but, if you want them in truth, says John, do not seek
them directly; on the contrary have a propensity towards
their opposite. You will find them in forgetting yourself and
your own satisfaction and seeking God's will alone. We find
ourselves by losing ourselves, letting ourselves go out in love.
So:

> That you may attain that in which you have no pleasure
> you must go by a way in which you have no pleasure.
> That you may attain to that which you know not
> you must go by a way which you know not.
> That you may attain that which you do not possess
> you must go by a way of non-possession.
> That you may come to be that which you are not
> you must go by a way in which you are nothing.

It is assumed that he whom we desire affords no immediate
pleasure, therefore to attain him we must be prepared to
endure the absence of pleasure. He is beyond our thought
and so the way to him is mysterious and obscure. As yet we
do not possess him. We feel this lack but must refuse to accept
a substitute. We can never come to our true fulfilment, our
authentic being, unless we undergo an undoing, a noughting.

We have an innate drive to seek our own perfection within
the dimensions of what we understand and consciously experience. We think we know what we need for our well-being and
happiness and demand this of life. This is very marked today
when greater opportunities are available. We say we must
feel fulfilled, that we have a right to this or that because we

46

need it for our fulfilment. We must not be diminshed or feel frustrated in our desires. But the truth is that we do not know what human fulfilment is. We can neither conceive of it nor the path to it except in Jesus and him crucified. To seek what we think is fulfilment, making it our sole aim and subordinating other people and things to our own needs is to lose our way. We must allow God to bring us to the fulfilment he has made us for, by a way that is infallible because it is his way for us. We must be brought to dispossession, emptiness, formlessness. A dreadful prospect? Does not this spell death to a human being? Paradoxically, no, it is the other side of the plenitude of life. It is to enter into him who is all, to be filled by the all.

The detached heart has a far greater joy and comfort in created realities, for to treat them possessively is to lose all joy in them. In the third book of the *Ascent* we shall find demolished any impression we may have formed of a harsh, loveless, joyless spirituality. John's path of asceticism is Christian. It leads towards the fulness of life, bringing freedom of spirit, insight, tranquillity. We learn to rely on God and not on ourselves. The whole created world is illumined and seen for what it is in a way the selfish heart can never know.[1] The unselfish heart alone knows the joy of pure love for others. The more another is loved the more God is loved. Nothing is evil to the pure. Generosity of heart, overflowing goodness, courage to face life and its demands, these are the fruits of true asceticism. The pure of heart enjoy a hundredfold even in this life, finding joy in all that is, be it human or divine. Creation is restored to its true form and becomes an unsullied mirror of the face of God.[2]

With the final paragraph of Book 1 John puts us on the summit of the mountain.

In self dispossession the heart is at rest.
It wants nothing.
Because it is grounded on Jesus

[1] ibid. bk 3:9.
[2] ibid bk 3:25.

47

not on itself.
It does not matter whether it feels
elated or dejected.

The asceticism outlined in these pages must be lifelong and
ever more penetrating and pure. It can become so only when
we receive the special help of God which John calls mystical
contemplation. This he treats of in the *Dark Night*.

5

Dark Night of Sense

The teaching of John of the Cross can never be understood unless we continually bear in mind that he is the doctor of mystical love and that his asceticism is only a preparation for co-operation with mystical prayer. John unhesitatingly uncovers our clinging selfishness. He makes absolute demands because he is so sure that we are not left alone, that God is always there intent on bringing us to the union with himself for which he made us. His presence to us in love has a twofold simultaneous effect – that of purifying and transforming. God does not purify us through some agent other than himself and then when we are purified come to us and transform us. His presence *is* our purification. The living flame, God himself invades us, but that which is supreme bliss is first experienced as purgation, for it destroys and consumes in us all that is alien to him. In the gentler imagery of the *Canticle*:

> When you turned to look on me
> Your beauty was entraced upon my face
> and so was I most dear to you . . .

> Ah! I was swarthy once
> But now all lovely in your eyes,
> Because you deigned to look on me
> And etched your beauty in my face.[1]

The image 'dark night' clearly suggests the aspect of purification as it is experienced by us, but we must never forget that transformation (or we could equally well say 'becoming')

[1]*Canticle*, st. 24–5.

is in exact proportion to purification. In the degree that fire dries out moisture it transforms the matter into fire itself. The divine gaze of love, even as it imprints its own likeness on us reveals most painfully our own swarthiness.

We can I think sit light to the division of the night into two distinct parts, sense and spirit. They denote one growth, not two separate operations in two departments of our being. The second book of the *Night* only develops and treats more intensively what has been said in the first. True, John reserves the term 'mystical contemplation' for the second night but it is clear that already he detects the first beginnings of it in what he calls the passive night of sense. *God* draws us out of the state of beginners, delivers us from a miserable, unworthy manner of knowing and loving him, sets us in the way of the Spirit. *God* changes light into darkness; *God* seals up the springs of sensible consolations.

It is John's intent to urge us to yield ourselves up to this action. For him the dark night of sense refers to a very early experience of purgation which shocks and upsets. It is passing in the sense that we grow accustomed to the new way and learn to accept trustfully what at first causes deep anxiety and distress. Any one who has experience of homoeopathic healing will have an excellent image of what is happening. The progress of a homoeopathic cure can be dramatic. Far from seeming better the patient throws up alarming symptoms: rash, fever, boils, sickness, headaches; as the body rids itself of deep-seated toxins. All the poisons absorbed through life are gradually rejected. It is a drastic but thorough-going treatment. In between the bouts of violent cleansing the patient knows periods of delightful well-being and imagines he is fully healed, only to be submerged again in another intense purgation. The dark night bears a resemblance to this. The purgation continues until everything that is alien to God is destroyed: there are times when it is experienced painfully and times when one can enjoy the relative health that has been gained.

We shall notice that the *Dark Night* is highly descriptive. Nothing can be said of the heart of the experience, the contact with the divine reality; this must, of its nature, escape detection. All that can be described are the effects and among these we must discern what are the essential effects and what circumstantial and ambiguous. The essential effects are three: a painful awareness of sinfulness, lack of satisfaction in meditation (that is, 'aridity'), and growth in goodness.

With John everything happens on a grand scale with high drama. His language is hyperbolic rather than literal. We may find it difficult to identify with his soaring flights and dark plummetings but these emotional states are unimportant and affect only some temperaments. However the 'come-down' following a period of sensible fervour is common enough whatever the tone of its emotional accompaniment. Very often there is a release of psychic energy at the time of conversion, a novelty and freshness as a wholly new dimension of being is opening up. We find ourselves striding like giants, snapping bonds we thought unbreakable, establishing with ease habits of prayer and asceticism. It can seem as if there has been a complete recasting of the personality. This is good. It enables us to break with sin and take practical steps towards a truly Christian life. But obviously there is something illusory in this state. Sooner or later the *élan* disappears, the engine winds down. We discover that our castle of virtue was built on sand and it topples. This is in no way due to infidelity nor to merely physical or psychic causes. Rather, the 'come-down' happens when, to the best of our lights, we are trying to please God.

John attributes this deflation to a direct contact with the reality of God himself. Contrary to what we expect, because our ideas of him are trivial, this contact is experienced not as delight, sensible sweetness and awareness of his presence but as a painful shock. A sense of our own misery fills the consciousness.

John unmasks the self-seeking inherent in our spiritual life. Pride, covetousness, lust, anger, gluttony, envy, sloth – the capital sins as they are called – are manifestations of our basic self-orientation. Every good person controls their cruder expressions but the deeply rooted self-orientation remains.

Only God can totally annihilate it. Although we may not identify with the temperament and personality John is dealing with when he treats of the capital sins nevertheless we are bound to recognise the basic egotism in ourselves. The faults he talks of may seem to us rather childish and naive, yet because they are blatant they are more easily dealt with. Subtler forms of vanity, pretentiousness, complacency, are more dangerous. Our very efforts to acquire virtue increase our self-possession. We base our progress on the immature assumption that we ourselves are the judges of what is good for us; that it is for us to set our own limits as to what is asked of us; that unless we do it all ourselves we will get nowhere.

The first effect of the divine encounter is a sharp attack on this self-seeking. The stronger-than-we comes to claim his own – and a hard time he has of it! In all sorts of ways, in the events of our daily life, in the lack of savour for spiritual things, he seeks to reveal our helplessness, our inability to manage by ourselves. Our very resistance increases our pain. We cannot trust. Inevitably we are basing everything on ourselves, our efforts, our success, our prayer and when these fail we panic. 'How hard it is to enter the kingdom of God.' Hard, not because we cannot rise to heroic deeds, not because some extraordinary feat is required, but simply because we cannot trust what we cannot see, understand, control. The kingdom of God, God's own world is around us; there is simply nothing to stop us entering into it save that we are lumbered up, so bulging with self-possession that we cannot squeeze through the narrow door accessible only to 'little ones'.

It is pitiful to look on, knowing well what is for another's peace and yet be unable to do anything. Only the persons concerned can say their own 'yes' to God's love that *is* peace.

I thought of how a man might stand beside
An iceberg's glassy wall, and hear inside
A wounded child, afraid and lonely, crying.
And how he would scrabble his desperate fingers, trying

To get through, break down, and all in vain –
The child still prisoned in its frozen pain.
Man, I thought is that child, and man the tomb
Of rigid ice that will not give God room
To save us and to love us and set free.
God passionately strives, but only we
Can break the rigour, let the life come in,
And, living now, true suffering can begin.[1]

How often Jesus must have felt thus. We must fix our eyes
on him, listen to him, ground ourselves on his truth rather
than on how things seem to us. We need to experience directly
that without him we can do nothing. It is a grace and we
should be thanking him, not moaning. Jesus has revealed
God's love for us, sinners that we are. He offers himself to
us; his whole desire, limitless energy is trained upon us to
bring us to our perfect fulfilment. 'If that is so, why doesn't
he do it?' This spontaneous cry is typical! 'I really am trying
and still nothing happens!'

It is obvious, yet strangely overlooked in practice, that
temperament affects our reactions. Those emotionally
insecure, with a low self-image, for instance, are going to find
all this much harder to bear than the secure person with
a proper sense of personal value. While guarding against
assessment of the reality and depth of a spiritual happening
by intensity of feeling, we must at the same time be ready to
acknowledge that there may well be a truly mystical experience underneath a lot of neurotic symptoms. God comes to
us as we are, through what we are. Everything can be taken
up and used by him to free us from ourselves and surrender
us to him. Ostensible handicaps can prove a blessing if only
we will trust that what is impossible to us is possible to God,
for 'everything is possible to God'.

In a similar way temperamental and circumstantial factors
can confuse what is meant by lack of savour in spiritual things
and the inability to meditate. This, as we have seen, is the
second effect of the mystical encounter and it is experienced

[1]Unpublished poem by Wendy Mary Beckett and used with her permission.

53

painfully at the point in question, greatly contributing to the sense of misery and failure. We must be warned again not to assess the reality with intensity of feeling. Pain, panic, drama, anxiety are in accordance with temperament and can have infinite variations. There are those who have never known what is commonly understood as sensible consolations and do not suffer the classic 'come-down'. On the other hand aridity, as commonly understood, seems never to have touched others. The majority perhaps, in varying tonalities, know both consolation and desolation and move from one to another. It must be borne in mind of course that here we are speaking exclusively of people in whom we detect the action of God.

The real point John is making is that at a certain point of growth a new form of knowledge is introduced that does not come through the normal channels of cognition. This is *real* knowledge of him who 'is night to the soul in this life', incomprehensible mystery. Thus in a practical existential way we are being asked to accept that 'nothing whatever that our imagination can conceive or our minds grasp in this life, can be God himself';[1] they are merely ideas about him no matter how spiritual they seem to be. Anything that we can actually regard and give an account of simply cannot be a direct experience of God.

> Do not be like the many unwise who, with low views of God, think that when they cannot comprehend him or be conscious of his presence he is then farther away and more hidden. For the contrary is true, namely, that he is nearer to them when they are least aware of it . . . When you are near him the infirmity of your vision makes the darkness denser.[2]

Beginners for John are 'those who meditate on the spiritual road', which means they are those who are totally dependent on thoughts and ideas about God. Now for all of us, whatever

[1] *Ascent*, bk 2:8.
[2] *Canticle*, st. 1.

state we are in, this is the only distinct knowledge we have; it is all we *can* know in the common acceptance of the term. When we write or talk it is always this kind of knowledge that is involved. But for beginners it is literally the sum total of their knowledge. It is not, as with advanced persons, merely that this is their *conscious* knowledge of God – it is, in *objective reality*, the sum of their knowledge. They are completely dependent on what their intelligence discovers of him and, as knowledge and love are closely intertwined, their love too is limited in this way.

At every stage we must as human beings use our minds to discover more and more about God so as to discern his will with greater clarity. But there is another kind of knowledge, secret, obscure, non-conceptual, for which we have the potential and which needs a divine impulse to activate it. This is what John calls infused or mystical contemplation. In the dark night of sense he merely touches on it; he is to develop his teaching later. 'Beginners' lack this mystical knowledge, the 'advanced' are imbued with it – more and more it becomes the 'ground' from which their conceptual knowledge springs. Two persons could be dwelling on the same passage of Scripture and have basically the same ideas. In the case of the beginner the ideas would be the sum total, whereas 'behind', around, permeating the ideas of the other would be the obscure, divine 'knowing'. We may know in theory that there is this other kind of knowledge because we have read of it in Scripture and in books on the mystical life, but we cannot *really* know it until it is given. 'Divine things are never known until they are really our own. We only know them when we have found them, not when we are still looking and working for them.'[1]

Acquired knowledge is satisfying because it is our own, a possession. Inevitably it gives – albeit unconsciously – a sense of power, control. We know where we are, what we are about; we have a sense of 'being able to do it'; in other words there is the implicit assumption that we can make our own way to

[1] *Dark Night*, bk 2:17.

God. It is only a case of going on like this, everything nicely under control, and we shall get more and more spiritual, know more and more about God, wax holy! This is illusion. Once again this cannot be appreciated no matter how much we may know it theoretically. Theoretical knowledge in its turn becomes just another piece of spiritual acumen until God 'touches' us; then our illusions begin painfully to crumble and we find ourselves left with nothing. The new knowledge actuated in the depths of our being, uncurling as the tenderest of young plants, is not detected. This is not a possession, it cannot of its nature be appreciated or enjoyed as a personal attribute. Incipient though it be it has effects, and one of these is to take some of the gilt off our 'God'. As the 'God' is really ourselves, our ego is wounded in its most vulnerable area. It is one thing to be asked to renounce our ego in dealing with other people and things, we come to appreciate that this is only commonsense; but surely our prayer, our pursuit of God, is unselfishness itself? Are we not trying to renounce ourselves, do good in order to please God? Well, we are about to be tested in that! Are our reactions prompted by the desire to please God or to have a spiritual life, become a spiritual person? In other words is our tenacious egotism operating in what is the most supremely satisfying sphere of all?

Good education is important. If we are constantly reminded of the true nature of prayer, that it is essentially God giving himself to us, that we are there to receive him, looking to him in faith and hope, that we must ground ourselves on his absolute goodness and fidelity and not at all on our own feelings, on what happens, the excellence or shoddiness of our performance: if our mentors show little interest in our interesting prayer life but only in the way we live; then maybe there is little or no trauma. Unfortunately the opposite is usually the case; false expectations of prayer are aroused and nourished. Such an orientation may make the beginnings of the mystical life impossible.

John's teaching is a gift of God to the Church. His aim is not to make us self-conscious, continually checking our position on the map. He is showing us the 'logic' of the truly spiritual life, writing large the consequences of the unassailable facts regarding God and our relationship to him as outlined in the beginning. The basic facts no one denies in theory, it is when we are invited to live by them that we baulk. In our practical response we clearly deny what we hold in theory.

It seems we are asked to let prayer disappear, surrender our 'spiritual life', have no control over it. Yes, this is what must happen. We have to give full space to the Spirit awaking within us, uttering his secret inarticulate prayer. This is true prayer. Even the best spiritual education cannot 'do it for us'. Each of us must choose to trust not our own subjectivity but the God of all goodness and fidelity as revealed in Jesus; he who has sworn by his own eternal being that we are his dearly beloved and that he is our own God who will bring us to perfect fulfilment in himself. In all other areas of our human existence we can try to gain control, manage for ourselves; in this we must learn the opposite, learn to let go, let another take over, one we cannot see, feel or taste.

It would be wrong to assume that what John speaks of as dark night has nothing in common with ordinary non-religious human experience. The image is not alien. How many pages of literature, how many paintings and songs have as their theme a dark night when what once had meaning now has none – when life's light has been extinguished, the heart bruised, the mind bewildered. Bereavement, disappointment, failure, old age and, on the wider scene, the threat of atomic destruction, these and countless other common human experiences engulf us in night. All of them confront us with our finitude, raise fundamental questions on human existence and contain a challenge to accept our human vocation, whether we know the shape of that vocation or not. Every human being is for God and an openness for God. It is not only around us who know his name that the sun is shining but around every single person, seeking an entrance. He uses every occasion to illumine us and his illumination is most often perceived as darkness.

57

6

Aridity

Aridity is a state of consciousness that lacks a sense of spiritual well-being. The things of God hold no attraction for us and we feel that we are failing in what matters most. Life itself persistently shows us up as unspiritual, ungenerous. What we must try to do is shift our attention from this subjective state and focus on a truth that is bigger than ourselves.

Almost always God's greatest gifts are wrapped up in the sacking of painful self-knowledge. When we 'got on well' in prayer, when there was satisfaction in the mass and sacraments, when we could talk inspiringly of spiritual things and others showed respect for our wisdom, we had no idea of the true state of affairs. Humility is acceptance of the truth about ourselves, not an effort to work up humble sentiments in spite of our obvious excellence! It is seeing and accepting the truth that we are not noble, good and spiritual. This acceptance of lowliness means more to God than all our good works and fine intentions. What seems like loss and deprivation of blessings proves the very opposite. God gives himself not in what exalts our ego, flatters our pride and self-conceit, but in what humbles us. It is not that God takes delight in seeing us abased but that what happens must happen. When God, all-love, love that in its human expression sheds its last drop of blood for us, draws close, the ego can have no part with him, it is the dead opposite of such self-giving love. The ego is then shown up for what it is in its distortion and ugliness. In its own estimation and in the estimation of other egotisms it had seemed fine enough. Now it is beginning to be unmasked and revealed as it is. We have a choice – to accept this unmasking, consent that the ego should die and so have part with the humble Lord, or turn away our face from him and reinstate our threatened dignity. We cannot have him *and* our pride and satisfaction. We must grow in faith (this is the subject of Chapter 7). In faith, believing, we can dismiss all anxiety and this will relieve our pain. If we learn to trust, accept our poverty, 'aridity' will cease to be aridity.

Someone writes to me:

I begin to see why you keep telling me 'all's well', and I understand what Thérèse means by, 'It is the blind trust I have in his mercy . . . there is my *sole* treasure.' You see *I* realise now what a blessing it is to be forced to become utterly poor and incapable – at least one feels utterly poor and incapable and unworthy – and to have your inadequacies pull you down day after day, to see your own selfishness . . . It *forces* you to turn to Jesus 'in blind trust', which means that you throw yourself at him and say, 'You do it with me . . . help me . . . I can't do this myself.' And you blindly trust in his 'mercy' which is to say that you utterly believe that you are *not* throwing yourself against a blank wall, but into arms which catch you and support you, and set you on your feet enough to go on . . . with love . . . his love. And so you can forgive yourself . . . and smile even . . . in time.

If these things which hurt and discourage so much allow this to happen then I think it is a great thing. For I believe that Thérèse saw that *this* is really the nub of the whole matter. I *instinctively* feel so too. Really and truly it is too good to be true, isn't it? Mourning literally turned into gladness. It seems suddenly clear . . . Things will cloud again maybe, perhaps they *have* to, because faith, to grow strong, has to keep being reasserted . . . It also means, incidentally, that one need never worry about being able to do things like loving people who drive you crazy, because God *knows* you can't and isn't really expecting you to be able to by yourself. In short, if everything being wrong is a sure way of forcing you to cling to him, then it's certainly not only worth it but the best thing in your life yet! (Hard to believe in the midst of it all!)

Another writes:

The Lord pulled a few carpets from under me the last few weeks and I went back to try and see how I understood and internalised the Little Way. What is it based on?

God's longing for us, his desire to draw us to himself and give us himself is greater than any desire we may have. We can trust his longing for us. He waits for our willingness . . . We cannot trust in our own weak desire and love to take us to God. We must place our trust and confidence in his desire for us. We have to give up the desire to have *anything at all* to be proud of – even our willingness to have nothing! We must face our radical need for redemption not necessarily because we are all evil but because the sin in us makes us irreparably blind and confused (like people caught in treacle who at any attempt to free themselves become more deeply entrenched), and really understand that Jesus not only gives freedom but also new life – a life we cannot attain by our own efforts.

These expressions of real insight forged through life's pressures say it far better than any theorising. *Real* insights such as these – proved real because lived out – reveal the presence of the mystical. Many of us can say lovely things about our weakness and poverty but they remain beautiful notions. What matters is living it and this can never be a beautiful experience.

It is painful to stand by helpless when another writhes, trapped in his or her own misery. It is equally painful, if not more so, to witness someone running away from the experience of poverty, for in doing so they run from God. This is not uncommon. Often such people are persons of stature and capacity who could give him much. Often they are acclaimed by others. They cannot see, because they do not want to see, that their spiritual image matters far more to them than God. Deceiving themselves and others (incredible our ability for self-deception) with the noblest pretexts, they put a distance between themselves and any situation or person that threatens this image and seek to be where it is safely maintained. When someone has taken such a step it needs a miracle to extricate them from their tangle of spiritual illusions. It is self-perpetuating. Let someone come along with the insight to see through the façade, someone who could enlighten and free them, such a one is avoided. John tells us that many people begin to receive the first touches of contemplation – that is, begin to enter the night – but less than half make progress. This sad fact has been examined at some length in *Guidelines for Mystical Prayer*, in the chapters 'The Bridge' and 'The Hold-up'.

The dark night of sense is a spark of love for *God*, devoid of self-seeking. It will show itself in the unspectacular, thorough-going, daily unselfing outlined in the previous chapters of this book.

It is, I think, a mistake to assume that because John gives signs by which to test whether aridity is an effect of the touch of God or not, that it is important for us to know. For one thing, we *cannot* know with certainty; the signs remain ambiguous and in need of interpretative application. Furthermore the whole movement initiated by this divine touch is to take us away from ourselves, from any security to be found within ourselves, so that we rely only on faith. Preoccupation with our position on the spiritual road is a form of selfishness. We have to remember John's context. On the one hand illuminism with its preoccupation with 'experiences'; on the other the reaction which stated that meditation was the *only* safe and proper way of prayer, everything else was suspect.

John is writing to reassure and console those who find themselves in neither camp. They have no 'experiences', lack consolation, yet at the same time they can no longer profit by meditation. Many of his readers would be deeply imbued with the notion that they were praying only when they were discoursing with their minds, eliciting acts, doing the work themselves. Yet now they feel repugnance for this. John has to coax them away from this attitude, encourage them not to force meditation but accustom themselves to receive in darkness and unknowing the new form of prayer rising up within them. He discusses this at length in Chapters 12–15 of the second book of the *Ascent*.

Nevertheless some will have a question. John is emphatic: just as it is harmful to persist in meditation when the time has come to abandon it, it is likewise harmful to abandon it too soon, when infused prayer is not rising up. How can one be certain? Is not uncertainty harmful, diverting our attention from God and making us self-conscious? God does not set us puzzles. There must be a simple answer. There is – and here I allow another voice to speak.[1]

The simplicity of prayer, its sheer, terrifying uncomplicatedness, seems to be either the last thing most of us know or want to know. It is not difficult to intellectualise about prayer – like love, beauty and motherhood it quickly sets our eloquence aflow, it is not difficult but it is perfectly futile. In fact those glowing pages on prayer are worse than futile; they can be positively harmful. Writing about prayer, reading about prayer, talking about prayer, thinking about prayer, longing for prayer and wrapping myself more and more in these great cloudy sublimities that make me feel so aware of the spiritual: anything rather than actually praying. What am I doing but erecting a screen behind which I can safely maintain my self-esteem and hide away from God?

In comparison Jesus is almost brutally practical. 'If you love me, keep my commandments.' Nothing about how we feel towards him, simply the hard test of practicality; what are we actually doing? 'Lord, teach us how to pray': Jesus never seems to contemplate giving a theoretical answer, going into the question of what prayer is and what our dispositions should be, let alone any matter of degrees or states. If you ask Jesus a question you get an immediate working reply. Not: 'before you pray' or 'in order to pray' but: '*When* you

[1]The remainder of this chapter is from Wendy Mary Beckett, 'Simple prayer', *Clergy Review* (February 1978), and is here reprinted with permission.

pray, say: Father.' And the apostles receive a demonstration of what the Son means by prayer. Perhaps the most challenging thing about this demonstration is its utter simplicity, or if you prefer, its reality, its objectiveness.

'When you pray, say . . .' Would not most have expected something about, 'say: I love you, Father'? Indeed Jesus did love his Father, with a love that was his passionate preoccupation by night and day, 'food' for him, what always moved him. But he saw his love for his Father as he saw our love for him: primarily as a matter of objective action. 'I do always the things that please him.' Prayer for Jesus was another form, the purest and most objective form, of that surrender to the Father's will. There were no subjectives in it, no feelings. He loved and surrendered to his Father when every instinct rebelled, as in the Garden, just as profoundly as when 'he was filled with joy in the Holy Spirit'. What I am trying to say is that Jesus teaches us that prayer is above all a response to God, and it differs only in intensity from every other response we make to him. It is never something esoteric, merely life at its purest. Our feelings, our likings and dislikings, all these are immaterial. Prayer is not concerned with me but with God.

The essential act of prayer is to stand unprotected before God. What will God do? He will take possession of us. That he should do this is the whole purpose of life. We know we belong to God; we know too, if we are honest, that almost despite ourselves, we keep a deathly hold on our own autonomy. We are willing, in fact very ready, to pay God lip-service (just as we are ready to talk about prayer rather than to pray), because waving God as a banner keeps our conscience quiet. But really to belong to God is another matter. It means having nothing left for ourselves, always bound to the will of another, no sense of interior success to comfort us, living in the painful acknowledgement of being 'unprofitable servants'. It is a terrible thing to be a fallen creature, and for most of the time we busily push this truth out of our awareness. But prayer places us helpless before God and we taste the full bitterness of what we are. 'Our

God is a consuming fire', and my filth crackles as he seizes hold of me; he 'is all light' and my darkness shrivels under his blaze. It is this naked blaze of God that makes prayer so terrible. For most of the time we can persuade ourselves we are good enough, good as the next man, perhaps even better, who knows? Then we come to prayer – and there is nothing left in us, no ground on which to stand.

Normally as we grow older we become progressively skilled in coping with life. In most departments we acquire techniques we can fall back on when interest and attention wilt. It is part of maturity that there is always some reserve we can tap. But this is not so in prayer. It is the only human activity that depends solely and totally on its intrinsic truth. We are there before God – or rather, to the degree that we are there before God – we are exposed to all that he is, and he can neither deceive nor be deceived. It is not that we want to deceive, whether God or anybody else, but with other people we cannot help our human condition of obscurity. We are not wholly there for them, nor they for us. We are simply not able to be so. Nor should we be: no human occasion calls for total presence even were it within our power to offer it. But prayer calls for it. Prayer is prayer if we want it to be. Ask yourself: What do I really want when I pray? Do you want to be possessed by God? Or to put the same question more honestly do you want to want it? Then you have it. The one point Jesus stressed and repeated and brought up again is that: 'Whatever you ask the Father he will grant it to you.' His insistence on faith and perseverance are surely other ways of saying the same thing: you must really want, it must engross you. 'Wants' that are passing, faint emotional desires that you do not press with burning conviction, these are things you do not ask 'in Jesus' name'; how could you? But what you really want 'with all your heart and soul and mind and strength', that Jesus pledges himself to see that you are granted. He is not talking only, probably not even primarily, of 'prayer of petition', but of prayer. When you set yourself down to pray, WHAT DO YOU WANT? If you want God to take possession of you then you are praying. That is all prayer is.

There are no secrets, no short cuts, no methods. Prayer is the utterly ruthless test of your sincerity. It is the one place in the world where there is nowhere to hide. That is its utter bliss – and its torment.

Bliss or no, it is terrible to live with, to face up to its simplicity. I long to tell myself that the reason why I 'can't pray' is that I have never been taught, the right books have passed me by, the holy guru never came down my street. Hence the eager interest in books and articles about prayer – all obscuring from me my lack of true desire. Hence the enthusiasm for the holy retreat givers, the directors who will serve me as irrefutable alibi. If there were more to do would I not do it? (I fast twice a week, I give tithes of all I possess . . .) No, I would not do it, I have no intention of doing it, but of course to admit this to myself would rack me with guilt. Remember the rich young man (Mark 10:17–22)? He had all the right words. 'Good master, what must I do?' And Jesus tried to jolt him into reality. Why use words like 'good' when you do not understand them? But he persisted, and Jesus gave him what the young man truly believed he was asking for. Jesus tells him 'what to do', and of course he goes away sorrowful, because Jesus has taken it out of the region of ideals and emotions and rendered his Father's claims in plain fact. 'Sell, give, follow me.' It was not what was wanted. Do you think this man went away conscious of his inner falsehood and realising that he was quite unprepared to look at God straight? I hope he did; but I fear he may well have been sad because the Master's claims 'could not' be met, that he barricaded himself down behind the excuse of 'inability' which he convinced himself he longed to be able to overcome.

If you desire to stand surrendered before God, then you are standing there. It needs absolutely nothing else. Prayer is the last thing we should feel discouraged about. It concerns nobody except God – always longing to give himself in love – and my own decision. And that too is God's 'who works in us to will and to effect'. In a very true sense there is nothing more to say about prayer – 'the simplest thing out'. However two practical comments. The first is that prayer must have time. It is part of our normal living, the heart of it, and cannot fit in along with or during other activities any more than sleep can. Of itself it must swamp whatever we try to combine with it. It demands the whole of you, to hold you in the consuming fire, and then you can go about the rest of the day ablaze with him.

There is a tendency today for people to say, with greater or less distress, that they have no time for prayer. This is not true. (Forgive me!) What they mean is they have not got a peaceful hour, or two peaceful half-hours, or even three peaceful twenty minutes. If that is the day God has given them then he awaits their praying hearts precisely under these conditions. They are testing conditions surely, but not impossible. Nobody goes through the day without here and there the odd patch, a five-minute break, a ten-minute pause. If you do truly want to pray, well then pray. Take these times, poor crumbs of minutes though they be, and give yourself to God in them. You will not be able to feel prayerful in them but that is beside the point. You pray for God's sake. You are there for him to look on you, to love you, to take his holy pleasure in you. What can it matter if you feel any of this, get any comfort from it? We should be misers in prayer, scraping up these flinders of time and holding them out trustfully to the Father. But we should also watch for the longer stretches which we may be missing because we do not want to see them. Many things that are pleasant and profitable, TV programmes, books, conversations, may have to be sacrificed. But you will make this and any other sacrifices if you hunger and thirst for God to possess you. This is my whole point. There is time enough for what matters supremely to us, and there always will be. The exact amount of time is up to our commonsense. For most people an hour would be the norm, remembering constantly that I am talking about simply being there: the quality is a question for God. Tired or out-of-sorts I am still equally myself for him to take hold of me. I will feel nothing of it, that is all.

The other practical point is: what shall I do during prayer?

(How eagerly people long to be told the answer! For that would make me safe against God, well protected. I would know what to do!) But the answer is of the usual appalling simplicity: stand before God unprotected and you will know yourself what to do. I mean this in utter earnest. Methods are of value, naturally, but only as something to do 'if I want to', which in this context of response means if he wants me to. I may feel drawn to meditate, to sing to him, to stay before him in, say, an attitude of contrition or praise. Most often I shall want to do nothing but be in his presence. Whether I am aware of that presence does not matter. I know he is there whatever my feelings, just as Jesus knew when he felt abandoned on the cross. What pure praise of the Father's love; to feel abandoned and yet stay content before him, saying: 'Father, into your hands . . .'

We cannot sufficiently emphasise to ourselves that prayer is God's concern, and his one desire is to 'come and make his abode in us'. Do we believe him or not? Of course I can cheat. If I choose not to be there for him, and since I am not yet transformed into Jesus, to some extent I can always protect myself from the impact of his love, then that is cause for grief. But it is creative grief. It drives us helpless to Jesus to be healed. We say to him: 'If you want to you can make me clean.' He answers: 'I do want to – but do you?' That 'wanting' is ever the crux of the matter.

Is there any way of telling whether we do want Jesus to surrender us to his Father? In *Gaudy Night* Dorothy Sayers has one character ask another when we can know which are our overmastering desires. And she is told: when they have overmastered us. This is a very wise comment. If God has taken you so deeply into his love that he has transformed you into Jesus, then you have indeed wanted him with overmastering passion. But if this has not yet happened – even if humbly you must say that nothing much at all has happened ('this man went home justified rather than the other') – it can only be because secretly, deep down you have not wanted it to happen. This is something you cannot help – these hidden desires that shape our course are beyond our control.

But they are not beyond God's control. His whole reason for giving us the sacraments is to open up these recesses to grace and change what we think we want into actuality.

Our actions show what we do in fact want – depressing sight, and sadly coexistent with emotional consciousness of wholly other wants. We have to hand this over to God, both explicitly and by immersing our poverty in the strong objective prayer of the mass and sacraments. There we have Jesus giving himself totally to the Father and taking us with him. Then we can almost see, acted out before us, what the Spirit is trying to effect in our own depths. Let him effect it – let him be God for us. Whatever the past or my fears of the future, here and now, O Holy Spirit, utter within me the total yes of Jesus to the Father.

7

Active Night of Spirit

What is faith? 'It is a habit of the soul, certain and obscure,' says John, quoting theologians. But he also sees faith as dynamic: it is a secret ladder by which we ascend to God, entering into interior darkness which is spiritual detachment from all things, be they sensual or spiritual. It is 'secret' because hidden from sense and reason, it is the 'way we know not' for it takes us beyond our natural limits. Faith in itself is excessive light, but it is experienced by sense and reason as darkness for these reach only to natural knowledge. Reason of itself can know nothing except in a natural way, the beginnings of which can only come through the senses. John however adds significantly that reason is gifted with power to transcend itself when it is the will of God to bring it to a supernatural action.[1] In other words we are endowed with that which can 'see' God but we need a divine impulse to activate it. Therefore John understands faith as our activity, but an activity that has come to realisation through a divine enablement.

We may have noticed that John does not speak of faith in the first book of the *Ascent*; he reserves it for the night of spirit. It is the characteristic of those who have begun to enter the contemplative dimension. Of course faith is present in the earlier stages but in an elementary form, no different in kind from the faith we have in the non-religious field. Perhaps we can explain it in this way. Our faith is based on a historical man, Jesus, on his life and death, on his disciples' experience

[1] *Ascent*, bk 2:3.

69

of him as risen. We are not asked to make a completely irrational act of belief: there are facts for the mind to consider and weigh so as to bring us to a decision whether or not we are justified in putting our faith in this Jesus, in his insights, his knowledge of God, his values. It is a human judgment and a human assent such as we make in our ordinary relations. Of course the gravity of the matter and its consequences give it a unique character: its object lifts it far above all other acts of faith, but *as a human act* it is on the same level. This was the case with the first disciples. They experienced Jesus in the flesh and had to decide whether he was of God or not and whether they should commit themselves to him. We see how fragile was this faith; it could not stand up to the over-turning of their conceptions of what should befall God's envoy, his *messias* – it could only take them so far. With the coming of the Spirit they received a new impulse, real faith was born, a faith that recognised God in the crucified Jesus and lived out this vision.

To commit ourselves to Jesus and to the Father whom he reveals means a deliberate choosing to move off ourselves, to refuse to stand on ourselves, to be our own judges of reality. We have to discover Jesus' vision and make it our own even against what our senses and reason tell us. It means trying to live our human lives as he lived his in obedience to the Father. Faith has no reality if it is not love. Love chooses. Love moves out of self to the other; it is a movement of surrender. Faith, hope and love: these are different aspects of the one human surrender to the God of love.

Biblical faith is not a mere intellectual assent to this or that piece of information, it is an act of the whole person surrendering to the God who calls in love, or rather, offers himself in love. It is the human 'yes' to the infinite mystery of love. It is obedience.

In so far as we live out this faith we are open to God. He can then communicate himself to us no longer merely through ideas and thoughts about him as hitherto, but inwardly, as his own self. The capacity to believe is energised from divine contact and is no longer 'merely human'; it is now theological

70

not just in its object but in its operation. There is a revelation from within, secret, obscure, that is not mediated through the senses. Though the pattern of the working of faith as human decision and choice is never superseded, it is, as it were, reinforced by a secret power. At first it was just what it seemed to be, a human act of assent and trust; now it is infinitely more than that. It is an act of such power that it goes beyond all distinct knowledge into the illimitable, to God himself.

There is an analogy for the mystical knowledge we are talking about in the common experience of transcendence such as comes upon us when confronted with beauty in art or music, for instance. It is a knowledge without form, inexpressible even to ourselves. We cannot hold it, it holds us. It is shy. Try to examine it, try to clutch it and it flees like the deer. We may seek to communicate our vision – this is what artists do – finding images and words, but we can never fully succeed. Images, words, form, become ciphers and that is all. What the artist achieves is another experience of beauty which, in its turn, can serve as a medium for what transcends it.

There are innumerable occasions when this shy visitant knocks: contemplation of the vastness of the universe as well as its infinitesimal constituents – mathematics, a flower, an insect, a human person, the encounters of love, death, disaster, to name a few. Such visitations we may call high points. There is a more fundamental, constant experience that we do not perceive. It is the experience of our very existence, and it is from this that all distinct thoughts flow; without this they could not be. All this is to show that we have by nature a capacity for non-conceptual knowledge. We realise such knowledge is not within our power. It is given and never becomes a possession as does distinct knowledge. It is obscure. These two words 'distinct' and 'obscure' we shall find constantly in John.

God is able to make himself known in a way analogous to what has been described above. Over and over again John insists that God exceeds all our powers, he cannot be known by the senses or reason. But known he can be. Revelation assures us of this and points the way. We can have full knowledge of God but not as our own, not in our control, not ours to manipulate. Conceptual knowledge is power, it is a possession. Mystical knowledge is something given, never within our grasp. Mystical knowledge has to do with absolute reality, with the unspeakable mystery of God. We are beings oriented to mystery, we are made for it. Human fulfilment lies not in a vast treasure-house of knowledge of which we are master, not in a laying bare the secret of reality, not in dissolving mystery but in the full immediate experience of it. 'The supreme act of human knowledge is not the shattering of mystery but its final assertion,' says Karl Rahner. Faith, hope, love, form one movement of choice and surrender to the mystery that has been revealed in Jesus as purest, self-bestowing love, Father. This is our ultimate bliss. How right John is to insist that we must journey in darkness, not trying to understand, see, taste so as to have power over God, but surrendering to him as mystery.

> When you dwell upon anything, that is, rest on it, you have forfeited All; to have All in all you must refuse to give your heart to anything. When you have the All it must be in its nakedness. You lose it if you want anything beside it or when you think you hold it as your own.[1]

'Mystery', says Rahner, 'is the sole peace of him who trusts himself to it, loves it humbly and surrenders himself fearlessly to it in knowledge and love . . . It is at once his menace and his blessed peace':

> It can make him chafe and protest,
> because it compels him to leave
> the tiny house of his ostensibly clear self-possession,
> to advance into the trackless spaces,
> even in the night.
> It seems to ask too much of him,
> to overburden him with monstrous claims.

[1]ibid. bk 1:13.

It forces upon him the dilemma
of either throwing himself into the unchartered, unending
    adventure
where he commits himself to the infinite,
or – despairing at the thought and so embittered –
of taking shelter in the suffocating den
of his own finite perspicacity.[1]

God is darkness in this life but a blessed darkness, a darkness
our deepest self wants. Anything less than the all, which being
no-thing, total mystery, must be darkness to us, would never
satisfy us. We cannot have it both ways: a God made to our
own measure, even our finest measure, whom we can grasp
with our minds; and at the same time perfect human fulfilment. Loyally we must accept him in darkness, refuse to
identify him with any means to him no matter how sublime
and spiritual these may seem. We must not try to drag him
out of his secrecy, but desire with intense desire to be taken
into it. Thus everything, natural goods, moral goods, spiritual
perceptions, illuminations, gifts of no matter how high and
rare a kind, the most lofty communications that can be
conceived – all these are things, creatures, means, and far,
far removed from him. Our tendency is always to turn them
into idols, substitute them for the impenetrable mystery. Faith
is therefore a constant stripping of what we understand to be
God in order that God may be what he is in his own reality:
it is a flight from where we are to where he is. It is always
an outward-bound movement that sets no limits: 'God, to
whom the understanding is journeying, transcends the understanding and is therefore incomprehensible and inaccessible
to it; and thus, when it is understanding, it is not approaching
God but is rather withdrawing itself from him.'[2]

We must not underestimate the difficulty we find in coming
to true faith. We may have no hesitation in being sure of our
faith while we think it consists in believing such and such a

[1]Karl Rahner, 'The concept of mystery in catholic theology', *Theological
Investigations*, vol. IV (1974).
[2]*Living Flame*, st. 3.

dogma held by the Church as revealed by God, or being able to recite the creed week after week in the eucharistic assembly. But when confronted with the reality of these truths as they touch us in our daily lives it is a different matter. As already said, no one questions that only Jesus has seen God, that the Father dwells in inaccessible light, yet how many of us face up to the full implications of this?

We are so loath to surrender ourselves to that over which we have no control whatsoever. The atheist in us all refuses to be what we are, a for-God-ness, and maintains its claim to be for itself. This is the fundamental disobedience, the basic sin. Natural religion tries to control God and, Christian though we are, we still carry within us the natural man. In Scripture this is the 'world' over which the father of lies holds sway; a realm that shuts itself off from God and chooses to exist within its own boundaries, subject to its own definitions and its own will.

How profoundly John of the Cross understands all this. He is going to display Jesus Christ before our eyes to shock us into seeing how different are our human views and what we think are such spiritual, holy attitudes, from his. But let us revise a little. At the beginning it was essential to make every possible use of good thoughts, ideas, impressions, to help us to choose to follow Jesus. We needed to live with these, savour them, treasure them. Their attraction, the interest they aroused and the satisfaction they afforded enabled us to renounce to some extent self-indulgent ways and grounded us in good habits of frequenting the sacraments, prayer and other spiritual works. Then sooner or later a reaction, a 'come-down' sets in which is the effect of God's direct action and by which he weans us from low, totally inadequate ways of approaching him. In Book 2 of the *Ascent* John deals with those who have come to a certain reformation of their lower nature which is now purer, freer and able to respond should God 'touch' them. There is no holding God back once the way is free for him and it is John's aim to show us how to clear the way and keep it clear. He is going to point out all manner of obstacles that we would never have dreamed of as obstacles; rather, we would have concluded they were truly divine communications. John saw as perhaps no one else had seen (at least no one who has given us their insights) how detrimental are these spiritual obstacles, and that there is scarcely anyone who has not suffered great losses through them.

In his day, as already said, the view prevailed almost unchallenged that the spiritual life consisted in all manner of 'favours'; these *were* the mystical life and the higher the favours the more profound the union with God. Not only this, he witnessed positive gluttony for pleasurable experiences, saw that these were what supposedly spiritual people were really seeking and even the best of them were hardly free from all such greed. We cannot deny that John's teaching is polemical and, inevitably, this will lead him to overstatement from time to time, but his essential point remains valid.

John explains to us in what union with God consists, how it has nothing to do with 'experiences'. It is a union of conformity. God dwells, is substantially present, in every human being, 'in him we live and move and are' (Acts 17:28). John calls this God's natural presence by which he holds all things in being. This is essential union but it is meant to become a union of love, of likeness. God desires with all the energy of his being to bring about such a union of love and this can only be by his communicating himself. He alone can effect this union but we must prepare ourselves. Our work is to clear away obstacles, abdicate from our own self-possession. We can never get hold of God, we can never make ourselves like him so as to win his favour. As we have tried to express, everything we have by way of distinct knowledge and experience of him, everything we can look at, claim as ours, is not and cannot be he, therefore it must be renounced. We must see these things for what they are, creatures, possible means to him, but far removed from him in actuality.

No creature can by any action of its own attain to that which is God and therefore we must be detached from all created things, from all actions and powers of our own, from our own understanding, liking and feeling, so that passing by everything which is unlike to and not in conformity with God, we may be open to receive him as he is and be conformed to him by this living contact; resting on nothing that is not he so that we may be transformed by him. When we see him we shall become like him because we shall see him as he really is.[1] But on the whole we are not satisfied with that. We crave for a glimpse of his face, revelations of him which indicate we are close to him, that make us feel we are spiritual and holy, that lift us up and fill us with exalted sentiments. The more we rely on our own selves, on what we are, what we have attained; the more inflexible we become, not recognising the way he comes to us but insisting on the safe, secure ways *we* know; then the less we resign ourselves into the only hands that can lift us up to him.

John illustrates his teaching with an image. We are like windows: divine light – the natural presence of God – is there always beating on the panes, but the panes are dirty, so dirty that the light cannot penetrate. Our task is very simple indeed: 'God, like the sun, is above us, ready to communicate himself to us.'[2] We do not have to make the sun shine, we have not to create our little suns, all we have to do is let the sun in and this we accomplish by cleaning the windows. When they are free from every stain the pure unadulterated light pours in. Then the window cannot be seen; it is all one with the light and, in its own way, has become light and light-giving.

In Book 1 of the *Dark Night* John shows us how the mud is removed from the windows, but that is not enough. We might think our windows are clean and that the sun is shining through. John sees they are not clean, and that as yet we do not even know what light is. In our present book (the *Ascent*) he shows us the films and dirty stains that still remain – the stains of attachment to our own understanding, tasting, feeling, imagining in regard to God. What is needed is great purity of heart, selflessness and trustful abandonment. John

[1]See *Ascent*, bk 2:5.
[2]*Living Flame*, st. 3.

sees that the function of the three theological virtues, faith, hope and charity, is to bring us to purity of heart. Faith ensures that we do not rest in anything we can understand but remain in darkness; hope replaces self-possession and all supposed achievement; charity compels us to love God above all things. If we want to make progress, to respond fully to the grace we are beginning to receive, then all our intent must be to develop these three virtues. For all practical purposes we do not need to make any distinction and the word faith will cover all, denoting the proper response of the whole person to God.

We must labour ourselves to enter into the night of faith. This is John's immediate preoccupation. He takes up the words of Jesus that have impressed him so much: 'How narrow is the gate and strait the way that leads to life, and few there are that find it.' He cannot emphasise enough how empty, how detached we must be to attain to 'life'; how different the way from that which we imagine. Our Lord himself expressed the same frustration with his apostrophe 'how': '*How* narrow the gate'; that is, much narrower than you think! This gate in John's interpretation is the night of sense when we must detach ourselves from the things of time and sense. The strait way relates to the night of the spirit and 'few there are that find it'. This John sees for himself. There are few who understand and really want to enter into this ultimate detachment and emptiness of spirit.

> Enter in at the strait gate:
> for wide is the gate
> and broad the way
> which leads to destruction
> and many go in thereat:
> because
> strait is the gate
> and narrow is the way
> which leads to life,
> and few there are that find it. (Matt. 7:13–14)

The many simply 'go in' by a way that is *obvious*. The word for 'broad' is related to the image of something right out in the open; whereas those bound for life have to *find* the way to life. Thus we have two types of travellers: the one aimless, letting the broad way choose them, so to speak, indolent, stumbling upon the open road to nowhere and simply going where it leads; the other looking for the right road, the road that is by no means obvious or inviting and choosing it when discovered. Drifting leads to destruction. No one attains to life save by striving and choosing.

Two gates open on to two roads: the one is 'strait', narrow, confined, you have to squeeze through; the other is wide, broad, flat, easily accessible. The first image is of a narrow concealed mountain path, but not for a moment must we concede that God has made things deliberately obscure. No, to those who really want him, who are humble of heart, there is no problem. They recognise the road and instinctively walk upon it. It is our pride and self-sufficiency, our self-seeking, that does not want to see it, that wants to travel by the obvious broad way.

We notice how, following the saying of Jesus on the strait gate and way, we have examples of those who have not found it, who are stumbling along the broad open road. They are those who are in fact claiming a special relationship to God. They claim Jesus as Lord, prophesy in his name, cast out demons and do mighty works. Nevertheless Jesus knows them not; they are not in him the only way. They are not building their lives on him but on themselves. They are not doing the will of the Father. The pathway up the mountain of perfection, strait and steep, demands that those who climb it carry nothing that would weigh them down or encumber them. We must seek after God alone; he must be the sole object of all our striving.

8

Contemplating Christ Crucified

We have a supreme model of mountain climbing in Jesus himself. 'If any man will come after me, let him deny himself, take up his cross and follow me. For whosoever will save his life shall lose it and whosoever shall lose his life for my sake . . . shall save it' (Mark 8:34–5). At this John takes wing, impassioned. His own words need no commentary, they speak with tremendous power:

> O that someone would teach us how to understand, practise and feel what is involved in this profound lesson of self-denial given us by our Lord himself, that spiritual persons may perceive how different on this road their conduct ought to be from that which many of them think to be right! Some consider any kind of retirement from the world and any correction of excesses to be sufficient; others are content with a certain degree of virtue, persevere in prayer and practise mortification, but they do not rise to this detachment and poverty, or self-denial, or spiritual pureness – all these are the same thing – which our Saviour here recommends, because they nourish and clothe their natural self with consolations, instead of detaching themselves therefrom, and denying themselves in all things for God. They think it enough to deny themselves in the things of this world, without annihilating and purging themselves of all self-seeking in spiritual things. Hence it comes to pass, that when any of this solid devotion presents itself to them, which consists in the annihilation of all sweetness in God, in dryness, in distaste, in trouble, which is the real spiritual

79

cross and the naked spiritual poverty of Christ, they run from it as from death itself. They seek only for delights, for sweet communications and satisfactions in God; but this is not self-denial nor detachment of spirit, but rather spiritual gluttony. They render themselves spiritually enemies of the cross of Christ, for true spirituality seeks for bitterness rather than sweetness in God, inclines to suffering more than to consolation, knowing well that this is to follow Christ and deny self, while the other course is perhaps nothing but to seek self in God which is the very opposite of love.[1]

Look at Jesus himself, look at him above all on the cross. The act which effected the union of all mankind with God was wrought when Jesus himself had been brought to nothing. How easily spiritual persons move away from him! We draw our ideas of how the spiritual life should be from this writer or that, this school of thought or that, but do not fix our eyes on the supreme Master. We could not fail to find and choose the strait road leading to life did we but keep our eyes on him.

The passion in Mark, when read with care, can stun us with its power and beauty. None of the evangelists refers to the physical torments: everyone of that time knew of crucifixion, there was no need to spell out the barbarous details. But in fact physical suffering was not their concern. They wanted to show the significance of this man and his manner of dying. How unbearable in its unrelieved starkness is Mark's account! Jesus' agony is pure human misery, horror, shock, fear. There is no heavenly visitant to support him; his disciples sleep; his life is bartered for a murderer's and the murderer's reckoned of greater value. No loving heart comes forward to help him bear his cross, a stranger is forced to do it. His garments are disposed of before death; he is naked. There is not a thing his own, not a person true to him. He is surrounded only by enemies. And then the mockery, the taunting and wagging of heads by the people, religious

[1]*Ascent*, bk 2:7.

leaders, his companions in torment. A pall of thick darkness cuts him off from the world he knows. Heaven too is obliterated. His one word breaking the terrible silence is a cry of unutterable desolation to the Father who seems no longer there.

Mark offers nothing to the senses, nothing to the emotions: on that level it was sheer disaster. A helpless man killed with not a soul to stand by him; his cause in ruins and he himself denied any assurance of God's sustaining presence and approbation. Only faith survives – Jesus' own faith which is not a matter of sense and feeling but of total commitment to the God he *knows* is Father, no matter how hidden, how unfatherlike he seems. Jesus utters his last cry and dies. No sign. Nothing to assure us of his victory. But Mark is sure of it and expresses it in a powerful symbol. The temple veil is ripped from top to bottom; the veil symbolising the separation between the all-holy God and his unholy people. Jesus' death has annihilated it; we have unimpeded access to God. We also see the miracle of faith when a human being is enabled to believe in this pitiful 'failure' – against reason, common sense, all the evidence of his senses: 'Truly this man was the Son of God!' (Matt. 27:54).

Such is the picture John of the Cross holds before us as the 'way', the way of faith. But let us look further. Mark's is not the only account of Jesus' passion and death. One account does not negate the others. Each writer is struggling to present his vision of Jesus and his saving death. Luke in no way denies anything Mark writes of utter desolation on the sense level. Luke's angel in the garden of Gethsemane is his way of telling us, 'do not be deceived by appearances; the Father is with him and Jesus knows it in the depths of his being'. He accepts all, it does not just come upon him and overwhelm him. His soul is in his hands. So much so that he can still be sensitive to others in their trials and sorrows. He looks at the erring Peter, speaks to the mourning women, and his words utter the truth of the situation: it is not me you should weep for, I am happy – in spite of all appearances I am happy. I am with my Father, doing his will. You and all in this city

are the ones to be pitied. We hear him forgiving his enemies.
A great salvific act is going on: faith is born, heaven is opened,
sinners enter. Jesus knows it. He is a king on the cross
bringing us into his kingdom. Jesus' last cry is to the Father,
committing himself into his loving hands. That is what death
is for him.

Here we see what it means to live in and by faith; what it
means for a human being to be united with God. We see
Jesus annihilated in all things, brought low according to
men's view, emptied out, enjoying no tangible proofs of his
Father's love and yet wholly one with God redeeming the
world. How we need to remember this and live from this
knowledge in our day to day lives.

It is John's gospel above all that expressly reveals Jesus'
dispossession of self. Jesus had no life of his own, no thoughts,
no views, no will. He affirms with all his being what it means
to be human, a receptivity for the Father, an emptiness for
him to fill. Jesus is pure transcendent spirit in constant movement to the Father: 'I go to the Father.' He is supremely for
the Father, from the Father. He is *the* man – 'Behold the
man!' – because of his total fidelity to transcendence. The
whole of his being was thrown behind this ecstatic journey to
the Father. It was not accomplished in one brief pregnant
hour, but day by day in the working out of his human existence, in his dealings with persons and things, in trouble and
disappointments, in searching for his Father's will. No words
can express how absolute was his dependence on his Father,
how poor, how 'nothing' he was in himself. It is precisely
from this poverty that he makes his stupendous claims. It is
the Father he is proclaiming not himself.

John shows us in Jesus what man is and what his destiny,
nothing less than to be Son of God. Because Jesus is emptied
out the Father is free to give himself as he wants to, totally
and without measure. Thus everything the Father is Jesus is;
everything the Father does Jesus does. Jesus' self-emptying
love attained its completion on the cross: 'It is consummated,'
and was in itself the human expression of the Father's love.
We learn here that the very essence of the Father is to be

self-giving love, a love that keeps nothing back, that is totally ecstatic. We see what we could never have dreamed of, omnipotence that operates only in weakness and self-sacrifice. Oh, where is the God of glory that our pride so desires! No wonder that if we would reach our fulfilment in the mystery of a love such as this we must walk in ways we know not, must allow ourselves to die to our own selfish, limited, earthly ideas and permit ourselves to be led unknowing into the darkness which is in reality the radiant light of a love too pure for our self-reflecting eyes.

John of the Cross's doctrine (how aptly he is named!) is thoroughly christocentric. It would make no sense whatever without this vision of Jesus crucified, at once the expression of human transcendence and the self-expending love of God. Only this makes sense of the way of abnegation he demands, of the darkness in which we find ourselves. He is showing us how to enter into this mystery of mutual surrender. He would have us lay aside our own desires, our own ideas and visions, our own will, and abide 'blindfolded' in Jesus; content to be ignorant and helpless, trusting ourselves to Jesus who sees the Father, who truly knows him as he is in himself.

It was the very love of the Father that pressed Jesus to die of love for us; his heart was beating with the Father's love. This is what we must long for, this selfless love of Jesus. Jesus crucified is the dark night into which we must enter so as to be one with God. We must allow ourselves to be drawn into mystery.

So the way to God is not by acquisition, not by building ourselves up, not by understanding but by letting go. God himself will illumine our blindness, and this obscure knowledge is called mystical theology, the secret wisdom of God. We must renounce all clear perceptions of him and rest on faith alone. Faith alone unites us to God; it is that journey of trancendence which leaves self so as to attain to God. We have seen in Jesus the form it takes in this mortal life.

To understand John's thought as he proceeds through the second book of the *Ascent* we need to be standing on his vantage point. It was his experience – we have no means of knowing how wide this was or how many persons he actually knew with such intimacy – that when the night of sense was over (and it could last many years) there normally followed a period of refreshment when a person received consolations of a higher, more spiritual kind. Let us remind ourselves how suspicious we need to be of such generalities, yet unless we look from John's point of view we cannot understand the basic principles underlying his empirical approach.

The class of people he had in mind when he wrote his chapter on the spiritual nakedness of Christ were not in a state of desolation; spiritually speaking they were having a good time. John sees it as a perilous time when they are in danger of going backwards rather than forwards. Meticulously, systematically, as is his wont, he discusses various ways of apprehending and understanding the manner in which we attain knowledge. Of this he makes two divisions – 'natural' and 'supernatural'. 'The first includes all the means by which the understanding receives knowledge, whether through the channels of bodily senses or by reflection. The second comprises all that is beyond the natural powers and capacity of the understanding.'[1] It is the 'supernatural' that is under discussion here; we have already touched upon the first in Chapter 5. John says that supernatural knowledge is also of two kinds, one distinct and specific, the other confused, obscure, general. The latter is pure contemplation, the work of faith to which we open ourselves with a longing heart. John's deep concern is with the 'spiritual supernatural knowledge' that is distinct and specific. He wants it to fulfil its purpose and lead us to God, whereas in his sad experience it often seems to do the opposite and fosters egotism. Let us see his characteristic way of dealing with the issue.

John was writing at a time when there was much anxiety about the origin of 'favours', distinct 'supernatural knowledge' which he categorises as 'visions, revelations, locutions and spiritual impressions'. It was assumed that such were beyond the natural powers, but was there any assurance they

[1]ibid. bk 2:10.

were of God? Could they not have another source, the devil? No doubt the question was real because there was clear evidence that such 'favours' did not always lead to greater holiness but to spiritual pride, arrogance, sensuality. It was impossible to conceive that anything coming from God could have such effects. This put a large question mark over the spiritual experiences which abounded at that time. One has only to think of Teresa's anxieties, which were aggravated by the uncertain and insecure judgments of those she consulted. John side-steps the question. He does not attempt to discern the origin of 'favours' nor does he want his readers to waste time doing so. Perhaps here is revealed an insight he could scarcely express to himself. Did he not intuitively discern that which we of the post-Freudian age are fully aware of: that our *felt* reactions ('visions, revelations, locutions and spiritual impressions') come from ourselves, and *everything depends on us* as to whether they are 'of God' or 'of the devil'. We are told that Jesus was driven by the Spirit into the desert to be tempted by the devil. His temptations were 'from the devil' but he used them to give himself more fully to the Father; hence the apparent paradox 'driven by the Spirit'. It is typical of John that he would not have us waste a moment on what is non-essential. We are climbing up the mountain by the straight path of 'nothing'.

What then do we learn? Discernment must be focused on our *use* of 'favours'. What is arising from our deep egotism, guilt, fears, pride, must be sacrificed and handed over in love to God. We can be 'devil' to ourselves. What springs from the desire for God, which he himself has written into our being, must likewise be surrendered to him since *only he* can fulfil the desire – not impressions, not 'feelings', not spiritual elevations, but only 'pure God'. In either case the destructive thing is to apply the experience to oneself and bask in it. 'Favours' can play a very positive role in our ascent to God provided they are used properly. They are meant to propel us Godwards and be wholly 'of God'. It is the end that matters and John is pointing out that we can frustrate the end through misuse of the means, getting trapped in self-complacency, in what we take as proofs of our spirituality, whereas 'favours' are meant to draw us away from self and into God in practical deeds of love and unselfishness. We must beware of giving them an overwhelming significance, making them into *special* tokens of the divine love and presence far outweighing any others.

When God communicates himself it is in the depths of secrecy and we receive him passively. Once again John uses the image of a window. A clean window simply cannot obstruct the sun; by being itself it receives it. A natural, what we might call 'reflex action' of the human psyche, is to conceptualise, interpreting what has happened deep within in terms familiar to us. The danger is that of mistaking the human 'creation' for the divine. Whatever is *clearly perceived* must be renounced, not in the sense of being rejected or disregarded, but estimated correctly as a *means*. As already said, John has witnessed over and over again how even advanced persons suffer enormous losses through misuse of 'favours'. He expresses it in his own terms. Someone is being led into profound solitude wherein God communicates himself and then the devil (egotism) takes a hand. His tactic is to interest the person in what he or she can perceive, experience. He wants them to make much of such things, hold on to them as proof that they are spiritual.

We have an inveterate desire for enjoyment, for something for ourselves and we seize on any pretext. Impressions of whatever kind they are delude us with the sense that they *are* God, *are* the divine communication. Readily the experience is described as a profound encounter with God. Though in the case of a truly advanced person we cannot say that such communications have nothing to do with him, still they are not he. This is what John means when he points out that we only perceive light when it hits up against something. Pure light we cannot see. So to our human way of thinking we have a great knowledge of God, a more profound encounter with him when we experience favours. Not so, says John; on the contrary, this very experience, in so far as it is made much

86

of, is an impediment. It thwarts the penetration of light. We must value the way of pure faith above all.

John takes up the same subject from a slightly different angle but basically in the same way in Book 3 of the *Ascent* when he deals with the purification of the memory by hope and the will by love. In practice, as we have said, there is no need to make a distinction. We can think of the memory as the faculty of possession. After all our thoughts would be disconnected if we could not remember, or rather there would be no thoughts at all. Memory ensures continuity, ensures the process of thought, the acquisition of experience, our own growing self-identity. It is this faculty that would claim as its own all that comes into it. The spirit 'possesses' by memory. Now John insists that we can never hold God as a possession. The virtue of hope is directed towards what is not possessed and it is this virtue which keeps us poor and glad to be poor so that we can receive all from God at every moment. Rahner points out that even the face to face vision of God in heaven is not held as a possession. We look to him in hope knowing he is irrevocably ours but only through his own continuing gift. His fidelity alone is our guarantee, his everlasting love. If this is true of the consummation of our Christian life then it must be true all along the way. Growth means an increasing experience of poverty. This was the human experience of Jesus as we have seen. He lived utterly poor, an empty infinity, and thus was able to receive all as pure gift. God was able to give him the totality of himself. What we speak of as the possession of God being our ultimate fulfilment is a surrender of all rights, the profoundest acknowledgement that nothing in ourselves can charm love from the beloved; the love given to us is dependent on itself alone.

Our innate desire is to have something for ourselves, of ourselves. Often enough what lies behind 'favours' and a preoccupation with them is a deep desire for assurance. We feel these things authenticate our spiritual life. They do not. Someone in the very early beginnings of sensible consolation could sincerely identify with experiences St Teresa describes in her fifth and sixth mansions. The gulf between the two

87

states is immeasurable but not necessarily between what is experienced on the emotional and psychic levels. Nothing we experience in the spiritual life is itself any guarantee. We have no guarantee except God's love and fidelity. He does not want us to have any but this. We turn from him when we make much of such things, when we crave them and welcome them. Too easily they induce spiritual pride simply because we read in them signs of great spirituality. We must be convinced they are no such sign.

The true signs of the Spirit are very different: an ever-growing selflessness in daily living, self-disregard in all spheres, humility, service, devotedness, and in the inmost heart a joy at being empty of all, poor, abandoned to God as he appears at every moment in whatever guise, able to recognise him when all the senses cry out that this is not he, this could not be he. It is just there that the pure heart sees the humbled face of love that never commands assent but will only ask and invite. The 'joy' in question here is not an emotion, it is a *choosing* to place one's happiness where it properly belongs: in the fulfilment of life's deepest purposes, which is only another way of saying 'pleasing the Father'. This joy is invulnerable. It may be accompanied at times by felt joy, it may not. Either way does not matter. This is Jesus' own joy that nothing can take from us.

Anything whatsoever can be turned into spiritual riches, even our trials, sufferings, anxieties and scruples. We can think that suffering and spiritual trials authenticate or give us claims on God. We can be fomenting these, inducing them, seeking security. Likewise any complacency in our virtues or moral goodness is a sure sign that as yet we are not contemplatives. The first effect of true contemplation is to reveal that we are not good for it shows us the clay feet of our golden virtues. True humility *actually* experiences that of ourselves we can do nothing. It knows itself as incapable of goodness and relies only on God to keep it safe and supply what it needs at each moment. It has nothing and hopes for all from God. This is the effect of profound grace, but in so far as lies within us we must reject all complacency and welcome every occasion which reveals the illusory character of our supposed goodness. These occasions will never be lacking. God loves us too much not to provide them. Our part is to accept them and let them do their work in us.

No one understood this so well as John's spiritual daughter, Thérèse of Lisieux. She carried his doctrine on spiritual poverty – the casting aside of all spiritual riches (the hardest dispossession) – to the uttermost. She said over and over again that she was positively happy to experience her weakness and wretchedness and she taught her novices to be the same. 'Accept to stumble or even to fall at every step, to bear your crosses feebly. Love your weakness. You will gain more by this than if, sustained by grace, you carried off heroic deeds which would foster self-satisfaction and pride.' Her sisters were to offer to God the sacrifice of never seeing the fruits of their efforts even for a whole lifetime; to pray, 'My God, I'm happy that I have no fine elevated feelings, but I'm glad others have them.' Similarly John says in a letter to a nun that spiritual treasures must be hidden away and left in peace. It is better that we do not know they are there, better not to catch even a glimpse of them. We are thieves to ourselves and we need preserving from our own rapaciousness. God does this by working in us in a very secret way so that we cannot enjoy or take satisfaction in what he is giving to us. If he sees that it is good for us to know his workings then he will show us, but we must not mind if he does not. We must leave it to him. They are *his* treasures, for *his* delight not ours. Our greatest treasure must be to have the opportunity of giving him pleasure.[1] What pure love!

This insight springs from mystical depths; more truly mystical than the lyrical rhetoric John indulges in at times. Yet how ready we are to think that the poetic flights we meet in the *Canticle* and *Living Flame* are the true mystical experience and what we are discussing is only the lowly way to it or the state of the 'ordinary person'. This is not so. Flesh and blood can produce poetic flights equal to any John of the

[1] See Letter 29.

Cross attained, but flesh and blood can never reveal the mystery of a love that accepts to have nothing for itself, to be reduced to nothing so that divine love may be all.

9

Mystical Knowledge

What is mystical knowledge? It consists in a certain contact of the self with the divinity. It is God himself who is then felt and tasted, though not clearly and distinctly as he will be in glory.[1] We must be careful not to interpret 'felt' and 'tasted' in terms of our sense experience. Here they are used in analogy. The contact takes place at the deepest level of being, in our very substance, permeating and transforming it. When God is able to touch a person with a certain fulness (again the term is used metaphorically) it can have immediate powerful effects, purging away deep-rooted imperfections that have resisted a lifetime of effort and imparting great and steadfast love. This should encourage us to go on trying even though we seem to get nowhere, hoping against hope. In the twinkling of an eye God can do all that our efforts could never do. But it is precisely our efforts that have allowed him to create a capacity, a sensitivity which can receive, endure and respond to such a profound communication. It is to receive these touches of union which ultimately effect complete, irreversible union – the mystical marriage – that John is preparing us for. Humility, patient endurance and love of God for himself alone, seeking no reward other than giving him what he wants, these are the 'acts' that properly prepare us for them: not prayer techniques, not introspection, not straining after 'experiences'. Mystical knowledge is not a flash of insight now and then. It is a basic all-pervading awareness that is part of a person's way of being. It is their union with God, and will

[1]See *Ascent*, bk 2:26.

91

of course be in proportion to the depth and fulness of that union.

John points out that this pure knowledge, when truly pure, is hidden from the understanding; indeed it seems to create darkness.[1] He uses again the image of the sun and the window. The ray of sunshine is seen not in itself but as intercepted by the myriad atoms and particles of dust in the air. The less of these there are the less is the ray perceived. If the air were completely free of any atom the ray would be completely invisible. Pure and simple light is not the object of vision. The same is true of spiritual light. Contrary to our assumptions it is purest, most itself when unperceived. Whatever is perceived, 'tasted', 'felt', and so on, is not the pure light itself – not God. We may notice when John is speaking of pure contemplation which yet is in some way 'tasted' he allows that the devil can counterfeit it.[2] What he is saying of course is that a certain kind of effect or overflow of a contemplative grace can be produced by something other than pure contemplation. This only reinforces his point that all that can be distinctly perceived must not be confused with God: it should be used but never rested in.

Much is being done today to help people form habits of prayer: books, training in spiritual direction and so forth. How excellent this is! Stress it seems is placed on impressions, there is an effort to evoke emotional response. The neophyte is taught to be aware of his or her interior motions in prayer, is encouraged to interpret them as means by which God speaks to the individual. This is possibly a way of putting people in touch with themselves and then with God. Well-tried methods of meditation are supplemented by psychological skills. Valuable as this form of direction may be at a very early stage in the spiritual life it could, according to John, be detrimental later on. This is where discernment must come in. None of us likes aridity nor the sense of psychological disorder that often accompanies it. The effects of what John

[1] ibid. bk 2:14.
[2] ibid. bk 2:26.

calls 'dark night', a direct communication of God to created spirit, are not different in themselves from painful psychic states springing from various causes. The therapist naturally rushes in to put things right, to take away the burden, to impart confidence and joy. The spiritual therapist could do the same and inflict harm. The person in question is not battling with a purely human problem, and it will be noted that, in spite of the turmoil, emotional bleakness and sense of diminishment, they are fundamentally well. Far from being directed inwards, to checking up on how they feel, they should be directed away from themselves, encouraged to keep looking at Jesus as best they can, understanding what is happening to them in his light. They have to go against what they feel and cast themselves in faith into God. It is this effort of faith that develops them both humanly and spiritually.

I question whether this distinction is always understood by directors and retreat givers. It seems that people who have spent many years in prayer with all that implies are invited to exercises similar to those given to raw beginners. In their humility and docility they undertake them. Some will experience their 'wrongness' and no harm will be done. Others, perhaps those who have received but a light touch of contemplative prayer with its consequent diminishing of sensible fervour, are only too delighted to have it restored again and readily continue the form of direction prescribed. This is for them to go backwards.

The relation between our human activity and the activity of God remains mysterious and delicate and is not easily expressed. There is always danger of stressing one aspect at the expense of another aspect. John puts the emphasis on divine activity and seems to deprive the human of relevance once the divine is operative. At times we feel we are being asked to live in a mental vacuum. This of course is a false impression. All the same John's own temperament and experience, the world-denying spiritual atmosphere of his times, do lead him to underestimate the spiritual value of human activity in the field of created reality. We must beware too of his lack of shading: everything tends to be black or white.

However we nearly always find an amending sentence somewhere or other by which we can interpret his seemingly
inhuman injunction in a more balanced way. For example,
he says the spiritual person must never treasure up or retain
in the memory the things he may hear, touch, taste or smell.
He must forget them, never reflect on them. But, he adds
significantly, not if he can use them for a helpful meditation!
Moreover such forgetfulness must never be extended to the
sacred humanity. This latter point will be considered later.
Here, related to the memory, is the same teaching as in Book
1: 'every satisfaction offered to the senses which is not for the
honour and glory of God must be renounced'.

John is teaching true recollection, directedness. In so far
as we can, all our powers are to be under control and used
only for God. In practice this means rejecting every memory
that in any way tempts us to sin: such things as the wrong
we feel others have done us, our neighbours' supposed faults
and failings, aspects of their lives which are no concern of
ours. It means sacrificing harmful daydreaming that would
entice us away from our present duties, and countless other
things of a similar nature. At the same time we must have a
liberal view of what can form a good meditation. We can
recall Paul's words to the Philippians: 'Finally, brothers, fill
your minds with everything that is true, everything that is
noble, everything that is good and pure, everything that we
love and honour, and everything that can be thought virtuous
or worthy of praise' (Phil. 4:8 JB). The created world is God's
and speaks of him. Every thought that is not sinful is essentially a God-thought and points to him.

This brings us to reflect on our initial dismay. Are we asked
to live in a void? Can a person become fully human, really
develop, following John's rigorous path of denudation? We
must bear in mind that he is talking of denying the faculties,
purging the understanding and memory, primarily in the act
of prayer. It is at prayer that we must be free to receive
whatever God wants to give. We must not try to do it all
ourselves, make our own prayer, estimate its reality by our
conscious awareness of what is going on. He is directing us

to a very simple form of prayer, austere and unsatisfactory perhaps from our point of view. We can hinder God's gift of himself by our busy-ness. At the same time John takes for granted that we shall always be meditating on the mystery of Christ. Sometimes we shall be led to do this at prayer time itself but most often perhaps apart from prayer. It must never be neglected.

Human nature has a multiplicity of needs. These are implanted by God and no one may choose arbitrarily to deny any one of them. God wills the growth of the whole human person – body, mind, imagination, affectivity. In the past, for all sorts of reasons, devout Christians and indeed all who would seek the higher things of the spirit pursued to a greater or lesser extent a world-denying policy. Only certain aspects of creation, only certain aspects of human nature were truly affirmed; others, if not condemned or ostracised, were reduced to a bread-and-water diet. Such an attitude is not Christian. Of course the Spirit of God was always at work, and where good folk were docile to his promptings they avoided the excesses of such an outlook. Nevertheless no one can fully escape the conditioning of environment. Devout people who denied themselves legitimate activities and pleasures for the sake of a profound experience of prayer inevitably compensated, for nature has its own in-built mechanism of compensation. 'Worldly' pleasures and interests were more than supplied for in the spiritual life itself: visions, locutions, conscious awareness of God's loving caresses, raptures, swoons, and so forth.

Voluntary renunciations apart, there were further deprivations imposed by the times. In St Teresa's day only clerics had access to the full Bible and at one point even vernacular translations of it were forbidden to women! Ordinary folk were dependent on priests for their theology, and how staid, how meagre it seems to have been! Where were they to find stimulation? Within their own psychic world. No doubt God made use of these human reactions to bring people to himself, for he never fails to care for his children; he can and will use any means for this purpose. But today we have no excuse for attaching such spiritual importance to what, after all, has a certain illusory character. We may not isolate one particular area of created reality (because it feels more spiritual) and claim that it is a quite special manifestation of God. The paranormal is not supernatural. The supernatural is above nature, no-thing that is.

John of the Cross's doctrine of the night is essentially christological. It makes no sense apart from Christ crucified who is the wisdom and power of God. It is what it is because God is who he is – self-communicating love. This we know and receive only in Jesus; it is something flesh and blood could never reveal for it runs counter to what flesh and blood desire. The 'world' does not, cannot know the Father. Jesus alone knows the Father; his eyes were on him continually and he acted out all that he saw. The burning love of the Father became his own impetus, driving him to total self-giving. At the beginning of our spiritual journey John bids us take Jesus as our model, bids us have an avid appetite to imitate him in everything, constantly meditate on him. When we have grown spiritually we are invited to a deeper intimacy, a deeper sharing. John points us to Jesus in the great act of redemption, stripped of all, emptied out, brought to nothing. If we are to receive all God wants to give us we too must enter into this mystery of self-emptying.

Even people who are relatively spiritual are often far from grasping just how central Jesus must be in their lives. We know theoretically that God has revealed himself in Jesus, but in fact we do not take it seriously. John points this out to his contemporaries and, we must remember, they are people whom he sees as having made some progress, who are called to enter the obscure dimension of deeper faith which is the only means of union with God. They have acquired some self-control and virtue and have passed beyond the restrictions of discursive prayer. Nevertheless John sees them acting as those who have not entered into the Christian dimension. They still approach God in Old Testament fashion by ignoring Jesus.[1] Such persons would be shocked to have it put thus but it is the truth. They seek for clear knowledge apart from him, they seek it in signs and tokens and interior assurances. They want to uncover mysteries. They disdain ordinary reason and the natural law expecting to receive knowledge and guidance direct from God. John is willing to acknowledge that at least some of the favours they receive are from God, but here they are exploiting them, using them in fact to evade the encounter with him in naked faith.

Instead of darkness and not-knowing these people want clear knowledge; instead of poverty and humiliation they want to possess secrets; instead of struggle and affliction they want consolations; instead of the hard labour of acquiring virtue they want sweetness in prayer. They are bypassing Jesus, settling within the confines of created things, managing themselves, basically seeking themselves. This is not to enter into the mystery of the crucified Jesus.

In former times God used various ways to enlighten us but now he has spoken once for all by his Son. All other modes of communication are abolished. Formerly God could not make himself understood; there was no one of sufficient transparency to receive him. Now there is. Jesus is the definitive revelation of God; God has nothing more to reveal. You crave to know, be reassured, have a guarantee? Jesus will satisfy it. You look within at your own subjective feelings but what do they tell you? They can give no certitude. You have all the guarantee you need in Jesus. See what he has shown us of the Father's steadfast love, of his will to give us everything. See how he reveals the Father as total forgiveness. What need have you of further reassurance? You seek to know how to please God in all you do – then look to Jesus. There is scarcely anyone who does not depart from the way of pure faith and seek some personal, subjective, special revelation or assurance. There is no greater security, consolation or happiness than to lean absolutely on Jesus the man. John speaks of him as Christ-Man, stressing the humanity of the Lord. He is our

[1] ibid. bk 2:22.

brother, master, companion, yet we are not content with this precious gift, the all of God. When we truly know Jesus we have nothing to desire by way of signs or revelations. We do not need extraneous words of comfort. We know we have all the comfort of God in Jesus. If Jesus is our life then we cannot rest in the security of *feeling* that he is, feeling that it is all true. Faith allows for no rest or security anywhere, it stands steadfast alone. By definition there is no proof in faith, so what we feel is of little account. We *know*, which is another way of saying Jesus knows, and we accept to sacrifice our human longings to experience this knowledge because here on earth it is too much for us: 'You cannot bear it now.' To cling to Jesus, to be drawn by him into his own poverty and self-emptying, is to be drawn into the depths of God.

Until the very last stage of all, the state of spiritual marriage, there is always the danger of bypassing Jesus. We can still find the rawly human a scandal, and the crucified Christ anathema, even though we hail him with our minds and lips. In the last stage this is impossible. The perfect are one with Jesus, inseparable from him; he *is* them – their way, their truth, their life. A living knowledge of Jesus is the very heart of union. This deep knowledge is mystical, infused, but the loving heart goes on seeking to know more and more, chiefly through Scripture. 'There are in Christ depths to be fathomed. He is an inexhaustible mine with many recesses full of treasures, and however deeply we descend we shall never reach the end.'[1] Such knowledge as this is living, springing as it does from a sharing in his self-emptying.

Thanks to modern scientific methods we today have the possibility of a very privileged knowledge of Scripture, more true to the intention of the original writers whose work we now read in its necessary historical context. Formerly direct access to the Scriptures was the preserve of the few; now it is possible for all. The early Fathers and later monastic writers were soaked in it and references explicit or implicit underlie every page they wrote; but they lacked what is now available

[1] *Canticle*, st. 37.

to us if we would take the trouble to use it. If we too are steeped in this precious revelation we will have little need for 'experiences'; they will seem trivial and empty compared with the riches of Scripture. But we must bring to our study an explicit faith. This is God's chosen, humble way of communicating with his children. We apply our minds and hearts, we do what we can, but as always our part, though essential, does not 'do' it; it enables God to 'do' it. He needs this work as sticks are needed for a fire. Sticks are not fire and never create fire. On the other hand fire has to have something to enfire. What is more, mystical knowledge needs the distinct apprehension that flows from thought and reflection. The word of Scripture points to the mystery, shows us how to enter and be taken into it. The word, when the heart is prepared, communicates the silent presence of the mystery that is love.

It is not uncommon for some people who have reached a degree of interiority, have had 'experience' of the numinous or been gripped by an awareness of mystery, to eschew all visible and organised aspects of religion. Such things seem to them unworthy, irrelevant and puerile. What have these miserable little ceremonies to do with the ineffable? Something of this attitude can pervade the would-be contemplative. Outward forms can seem far less spiritual than what we experience in the silence of our room or in field and forest. We may secretly assume that outward forms are for the 'ordinary Christian', not for us who have become spiritual and special. Nobody would ever voice such a statement even to themselves, so much does it smack of conceitedness, but perhaps it is not totally absent from our inmost heart? It can arise from a lack of understanding; more often it is a symptom of pride and the deep human conviction that we can go to God ourselves. The sacramental liturgical life expresses the fundamental truth on which the Christian existence is based, namely, 'No one comes to the Father but by me.' It is God himself in Jesus who has given us our means of reconciliation, worship and reparation. The idea will always persist that we do not need a mediator; we worship in spirit and in truth.

But the great central act of our religion is not of our devising, it is given to us. We do not have to make our worship; we enter into, claim as our own, a worship God himself has given to us. God has done and does everything for us; all is pure grace. The sacraments affirm this.

Never are we more truly Christian than when we approach the sacraments with the Christian community. This is where God 'touches' us. Here, at this moment, is our guarantee. What need have we of a word spoken inwardly when we hear the word spoken outwardly: 'My body for you', 'Your sins are forgiven'. Our religion is historical; earthly because divine. God affirms the whole of our human being, wants it all, sanctifies it all, comes to us through its reality. In our sacred liturgy we have the concrete certainty of divine encounter and action. We are grounded on objectivity rather than on the quicksands of our poor subjectivity which can in certain states seem so sure, so divine.

Mysticism has everything to do with reality – the reality of God and the reality of man. God so loved the world that he gave his own Son to it and we too must love the world. Earlier John spoke of the active and passive night of sense as purifying the inward faculties to enable them to see the world in its sacred depths and meet God in it (this is what he means though his language is in the terminology of 'favours'). We should therefore welcome what is known as secularisation. In itself it is right, something God wants. It is a purification, a dark night of religion which allows a real and living faith to emerge.. Only too often what we think of as faith is simply shutting our eyes to three-quarters of reality lest it disturb (if not destroy) our so-called 'faith'. True faith never takes its gaze off reality, seeking in it always the face of God which it *knows* is there. It does not decide for itself the categories and forms his manifestation must take; he is acknowledged as sovereign Lord, *always* offering himself in love.

Science, materialism, atheism do not banish God; they clear the atmosphere for true faith. We can no longer confine God within the sacral and treat with him there. We must see him in all that is or not at all. If we are weak in faith we may find his seeming absence unendurable, the effort to seek him in the world with all its attendant risks unbearable, and so we retreat into a ghetto, building up for ourselves a little world of spiritual make-believe which is safe, comfortable, unchallenged. This is a powerful allure for some. It seems that *this* is the sphere of the holy where God really is, whereas secularity is unholy and must be shunned. If we would go forward, if we would surrender to God we must keep our doors wide open. We must trustingly deal with the world, love it, enjoy it. If we cling to our pietistic inwardness with its comforting illusions of love for God and intimacy with him we shall never find him fully. We shall have missed the strait gate and path and, contrary to what we think, be walking on the broad and obvious way, preferring our sense of security to facing the living God.

Substitute 'person of faith' for 'poet' in the following passage and we have an apt description of what it means to say 'yes' to the world of created reality.

His (the poet's) position at the hub of things is a position a man *takes* explicitly and for a purpose: to face 'the mystery of the universe', to face the world, to see the world. It is from this hub of things that the myriad objects are visible – those myriad objects that most of us stare at all our lives and never see. It is from this hub that the complexity of the world, that complexity which most of us succeed so easily in ignoring, can be observed. It is at this hub that the irresistible sweep of time, that tide which most of us take for granted and so never feel until it has all but carried us away, is felt as movement . . . the hub, in brief is not a spatial centre, such as the one illusion tells us we occupy, but a centre of awareness, a centre of receptivity . . . It is an ability to live in 'uncertainty, mystery and doubt' without any irritable reaching after fact and reason: without, that is to say, struggling to scramble ashore out of swirling, buffeting awareness of the world to those dry sandpits of 'fact' and 'reason' which keep the ocean off and so make seeming refuges for our minds.[1]

The created world emerges and remains suspended in the incomprehensible mystery of God and we must let ourselves be drawn into that incomprehensible mystery. True contemplatives are not concerned with themselves, not interested in their subjective world: they are occupied with objective reality.

All good people accept without question that they must be involved in the world in the form of other people's needs, in building a better future, counteracting evil in whatever form; the gospel message shouts loudly here. But perhaps not all appreciate the faith-fostering values of art and culture. Within our own 'desert' life of Carmel we foster the flowers of culture that are compatible with the desert and we see this not as an alleviation, a concession to less fervent spirits but as positive aids to faith and contemplation. Wide reading, art, drama – all within carefully controlled bounds – are accepted as part of our life today.

'Art is not an intellectual experience,' writes one of our sisters:

> it is too interwoven with searching and prayer to be pinned down in neat concepts. Modern art in Carmel is listened to and then the challenge is to try to live 'it' . . . I have grown up with a deep love of nature and the wild is in my blood. Not surprisingly therefore I can still vividly remember the first time I discovered Henry Moore – the sheer silent magnitude of his Madonna/Child sculptures and his wartime shelter and mining sketch books. His work has an extraordinary capacity to touch deeply primal areas in one's make-up. How these mysterious swathed figures echo something of every man's searching efforts to emerge from the dark, clouded world that seems to drag us back from freedom to respond wholeheartedly!
>
> As for colour and form: once I likened it to stepping

[1]from Archibald MacLeish, *Poetry and Experience* (1961).

through the wardrobe into Narnia as in C. S. Lewis's story and I cannot better this description. Though I passionately loved the Hebrides and Sutherland (how explain what it means to stand in such wild, desolate places?) I have *never* yet 'felt' the physical restraints of the enclosure or tiny cell.

Contemplation of an abstract work of art by someone like Klee or Kandinsky and so many of the post-war abstract expressionists (and by contemplation I mean living with a picture over a long period) throws open extraordinary vistas and one is simply *contented* by the creative genius bestowed on the human mind. A work of art takes two. Oh, the sheer beauty of thinking that I in 1986, through meditating on a work painted in another generation and time, can know in some small way that the reality of God in the world is confirmed.

It cannot be articulated as such, it is just known by the heart. It has to be personal knowledge taken into oneself and used. Art is a means to deepen our faith commitment, not a diversion which remains on an idealistic, dreamy level of living. If the reality of God is declared so emphatically in art, then this, with any revelation of God such as in litera-ture, has to flow by degrees into my life, my relationships, my responses, otherwise it is a useless distraction and could just be a way of brightening up the austerity . . .

The revelation of God in art can be very painful, exposing powerful drives to independence, but, as many times, art also certainly refocuses the spirit in times of hardship, often more effectively than the written word or conversation. We are left to express the totally 'other' by the only means at our disposal, namely contrast, light/dark, empty silences . . . See the work of Morris Louis where much of the canvas is blank. You are left feeling that the void is itself the subject, the inexpressibility of God . . . So often in these contrasts so expressed do we nor deep down see oblique references to what we sooner or later have to grapple with in our prayer and daily living? There is something we recognise, a visual image, a personal experience . . .

I find enormous wonder in the fact that someone who perhaps had no explicit intention of spiritual allegory in their works can create an art form – itself constrained by the artist's own limitations – so that years later I in Carmel can live with the painting, sculpture, whatever, and be taken *through* it. Yes, rejoicing in the colour and shape, but to a point where I know God *is* despite all sensible, confused feelings of absence, abandonment The creativity of the artist tells me God *is*.

Let it be said once again, we must not put too much weight on the fact that John of the Cross, in the second and third books of the *Ascent* claims to be addressing people at a particular stage of the spiritual life, that is, 'proficients'. If he is, then the stage in question covers a vast area, so vast as to be indefinable. It is far better to understand him as pointing a direction that is relevant wherever we are on the journey. He is always saying, 'No, it is not here, it is beyond,' and the arrow points always to obscurity. Our human lives here below consist of a succession of choices; we may never be static. We are 'active' even in repose. John gives a name to this human activity in so far as it is truly human, in so far as it is the appropriate response which brings a human being to its goal – faith. Faith is movement. It is the march of our feet towards our journey's end; it is the beat of our wings of transcendence, inseparable from hope and love. It is a going forth from our finite world into the infinite being of God. This fundamental choice is actualised in the thousand and one concrete details that fill our hours and days: duties faithfully carried out, acts of loving kindness, decisions for truth even in the smallest matters, self control . . . the list is endless. It is *living* faith that matters, not consciousness of faith, not a satisfying awareness of the security of faith. These may well accompany faith but they are not to be confused with it. The loftiest conceptions, the deepest insights are valueless unless they end in self-surrender to God.

In the *Ascent* John concentrates on our own activity, the steps we take to respond to God. God's activity John calls the passive night of spirit. To this we must now turn.

10

Passive Night of Spirit

> O night! that was my guide,
> O night! more lovely than the dawn.
> O night! you it was that joined us,
> Lover and Beloved;
> The Beloved quite transformed into her Love.

When we read the second book of the *Dark Night*, a work of
splendid poetry, we find little new material. For John the
second night is *the* night of which the other was but a faint
foreshadowing. Nevertheless in reality both form one
continuous night – the advance of divine love towards a sinful
human creature.

> The dark night is a certain inflowing of God into the human
> creature, which purges it of the ignorances and imperfec-
> tions belonging to its very nature. It is identified with
> infused contemplation or mystical knowledge of God,
> whereby God teaches it in a strange, secret way, educating
> it to perfect love. He does this himself; the creature can
> only be lovingly attentive, listening, receptive, allowing
> itself to be enlightened without understanding how.[1]

Our chapters on the passive night of sense and active night
of spirit include nearly all that needs to be said regarding this
second night. In John's purely logical structure the passive
night of spirit is towards the end of the journey or, to change
the image, it is the death throes of the ego before total
surrender in union. In so far as this is so, then to attempt to

[1] *Dark Night*, bk 2:5.

comment serves no practical purpose. When we are as far as that we need no guide and no guidance: 'God himself becomes the guide, and the way to himself. In solitude, detached from all things, having gone beyond all things, nothing can now profit or help the spiritual person except the Bridegroom Word himself.'[1] A way we know not, strange to all sense and understanding, cannot be talked of or written about; it can only be walked. Once we are truly established in this way we are safe: God is free to be our sole unhampered guide. Of the 'inflowing of God', infused contemplation, nothing can be said because it is God himself. All that can be spoken of are the possible effects.

Writing of the beatific vision which is, of course, the culmination of this 'inflowing of God', Rahner points out that it in no way involves the overcoming and mastery of absolute mystery. On the contrary the truly unfathomable mystery in all its finality and overpowering acuteness can now no longer be held at bay. It must be sustained and endured as it is in itself, without any possibility of escape into what can be grasped and thus controlled and submitted to oneself. The night is our learning to sustain and endure incomprehensible love which, in the measure it is welcomed, gives itself more penetratingly and fully. This love will hollow out vast caverns of desire and longing that only infinite love can fill. Few allow God to give himself thus.

John seems to imply that the passive night of spirit, understood as the final purgation preceding union, is an experience of intense terrible suffering which he likens to purgatory, if not to hell. Is such grievous suffering an essential factor of the passive night? Or to put the question slightly differently is there a fairly general pattern of what the experience of the night is *like*? This is, I think, a crucial question. To answer it we must recall the fundamental truth that the heart must be totally purified of egotism if we are to receive God fully – 'annihilated' is not too strong a term. Although we have to do all we can to deny our egotism wherever we meet it, its

[1] *Canticle*, st. 35.

overthrow can only be a divine work and it takes place in God's coming to us and our welcoming him. This is the essence of the night understood as purgation. It is the burning away of egotism, the death of the 'old man' and the substitution of the divinely human life, Jesus-life, for the sinful human life. What it *feels like* will vary enormously from person to person.

We can use the homely image of laundering. Essentially the purification of washing is the same, but different materials need different treatment. A linen tablecloth will 'experience' a most intense form of washing: boiling water, vigorous pummelling in the machine, thorough wringing out and hanging up exposed to wind and sun. An angora jersey is immersed in warm soft-soap water, gently swished, not wrung but patted tenderly and laid out in a protected place to dry. A camel-hair coat will be sent to the dry cleaners for progressive attention; it will know nothing of water or washing machine. Though all three are cleansed, purified, the experience of each differs considerably. We could say the linen is cleansed in a dramatic way with passionate intensity; the wool with slowness and gentleness; the camel-hair with aridity and in a manner hard to associate with washing.

Now John's descriptions in the *Dark Night* are more akin to the linen-washing process. Perhaps this was closest to his own experience. Maybe, as 'favours' in his day seem to have been of a dramatic kind, so also was the experience of purgation. We must remember too John's declared aim in writing the *Night*; it is to reassure and console people actually undergoing trials of one kind or another. It is John who has subsequently affected the whole tradition. Thanks to him we are prepared, at least intellectually, to believe that afflictions of the kind he describes may be an effect of the divine action, whereas the people of his day were not – quite the contrary! John therefore, to strengthen his point, draws on holy Scripture. He marshalls a host of texts expressive of great human torment and affliction. This, his argument goes, is proof that such sufferings are related to the Spirit of God; they come upon his friends. Therefore, no matter how grievous the pain, spiritual persons can be reassured. Possibly too, convinced of the importance of his insights and wanting to add weight to his authority, John tried to impress his readers with recounting the depth and range of his experience.

In our day the dark night seems to be more commonly experienced as a 'dry clean', a long-drawn-out greyness where nothing happens and where it seems inconceivable that anything will happen – ever. Is not this painful to our nature? Sometimes is there not a temptation to escape from this into dramatic sufferings? These at least give us a sense that something is happening, that we *are* suffering! It is by no means out of the question that the more dramatic sufferings are a device – *almost* unconscious – for making the drabness bearable. After all John and other authors of weight attribute such to advanced spiritual states, whereas who could possibly think drab grey uneventfulness denoted any such thing? An attempt to assess the reality and depth of divine purgation by the kind and intensity of suffering is erroneous. What we must hold on to is that God's purifying action is *always* effective in destroying *egotism*. This is real affliction whereas what we do almost always inflates the ego. True affliction deprives us of every vestige of self-complacency. It is often low-keyed, miserable, something we are ashamed to call suffering. If we strip John's descriptions, even the most poetic and dramatic, to the bone, this is what we find: a profound all-pervading sense of poverty, nothingness, meanness. Most truly the heart knows that it is not good, so far removed from God that it seems impossible that he is near, nor ever will be. As for feeling advanced, this is out of the question. It will honestly think it is hardly beginning.

Spiritual people are very quick to say and to think that they are nothing, that they feel poor, empty, helpless; but a discerning person recognises that these sentiments are only skin deep, very different from the state of one truly in the night. The vast yearning caverns John describes so eloquently have nothing poetic about them in real life, neither has the burning enkindling of love. Here is the mystery of a human person of flesh and blood in this workaday world, eating, sleeping, going about their business like every one else, yet all the time engaged in an overwhelming encounter with divine love, which on the level of ordinary experience is known only as an inglorious, unperceptive, unresponsive state. The profound secret knowledge of God can empty out the world for them so that they are left savourless on earth as in heaven. But we must never induce such a condition. This is an *effect* of a great secret love and a great secret knowledge. To attempt to induce a state of barrenness, savourlessness, would be to end up truly barren, truly empty and subhuman.

It is always important to maintain perspective. In our desire to show that the essential teaching of John belongs to us all, that he is, in his own way, unveiling the 'mystery of the kingdom' as it takes possession of an individual heart, we must avoid the impression that union with God is commonplace and that many persons attain to it. We do well to take John's assessment seriously: 'few' attain to the state of union in this life; 'few' undergo the dark night of the spirit understood as the last lap of purification. He gives the reason: 'in this marvellous work which God himself begins, so many are weak, shrinking from trouble, unwilling to endure the least discomfort or mortification, or to *labour with constant patience* . . . They lack "*resolution*".' And then once again John 'of the Cross' takes flight:

O you that seek your own ease and comfort, if you knew how necessary for this high state is suffering, and how profitable suffering and mortification are for attaining these great blessings, you would never seek for comfort anywhere, but you would rather take up the cross with the vinegar and gall, and would count it an inestimable favour, knowing that thus dying to the world and to your own selves you would live to God in spiritual joy. In the *patient endurance* of your exterior afflictions you would merit at the hands of God that he should look upon you, cleanse you and purify you more and more in these spiritual tribulations. They whom he thus blesses must have served him long and well, and their life be most pleasing in his sight . . .

110

This is the way God deals with those whom it is his will to exalt. He suffers them to be tempted, afflicted, tormented and chastened, inwardly and outwardly, to the utmost limit of their strength, that he may deify them, unite them to himself in his wisdom . . . It is very necessary for the spiritual person to endure these tribulations and trials, inward and outward, spiritual and corporeal, great and small, with *great resolution and patience, accepting all from the hand of God* for its healing and good, not shrinking from them, because they are for its health . . . remembering that they are few in number who deserve to be made perfect through sufferings so as to attain to so high a state as this.[1]

John will not allow us to think we can have God cheaply. We must needs give our all. *God* will do the work if we let him, and whatever he does, because it is he, can be borne. God never asks the impossible. So often we allow our imagination to conjure up in a vague, if not specific way, mysterious torments that surely await us if we give ourselves fully, and it is often this purely imaginary 'suffering' which keeps us back. We suffer far more from our imagination than from reality. The latter is received moment by moment and is always bearable. It is when we allow ourselves to project ahead: 'This is going to go on and on and I won't be able to bear it', 'This may happen . . .', 'God might ask this or that . . .', that we lose heart. It ceases to be his yoke and his burden and becomes one of our own making. John's real point, in my opinion, is the need for *resolution*. We must make up our minds once for all, renewing the decision countless times daily and hourly, that we shall let God have everything he wants. We shall trust him. Thus as each moment comes with its task, its encounter, its joy or pain, we see him in it and embrace him. Most of the time we shall not be conscious of whether we are suffering or not; we shall lose all interest in ourselves.

After resolution perhaps the next most important word is patience. Holiness is normally a matter of long, long patient

[1]*Living Flame*, st. 2 (italics mine).

111

labour and courageous acceptance of life as it is experienced at every moment. Each of us has illusions of one kind or another; we cannot help this. But divine love will gradually, or suddenly, divest us of them and bring us to live in naked reality, in truth. It seems to me that we should always assume there are elements of unreality in us and desire to be brought to truth. If we allow ourselves to think we have attained the end before we actually have, then without doubt we shall lose the sharp edge of desire and come to a standstill. At the same time we must have invincible hope that one day, most surely, most certainly we shall attain him.

God alone knows the inmost personal being and how it must be purified, he can be relied on. But means have infinite variations. Experience of his work in others leaves us amazed, awestruck over and over again at the subtlety of his ways. He knows just where to put his finger, knows the inmost fibres and just where the disease has grip. We can never see this beforehand for ourselves. We see it maybe when it actually happens, either in ourselves or others. We may have prayed with deep earnestness for God to purify us, to accomplish his work at whatever cost; and then something will come about, perhaps trivial in nature, that touches our most vulnerable spot, and we find ourselves saying, 'anything but *this*'; yet *this* is our tenacious ego.

> When you feel you have no desire for God, when your will is arid and constrained and you seem incapable of any spiritual activity, do not be upset. It is a boon, a good thing. God is freeing you from yourself, taking your hands off the controls of your life. No matter how hard you try, you can never do anything that is faultless and free from self because of your impurities and sluggishness. But now God is taking you by the hand and guiding you in the dark, as we guide a blind man, along a strange road to an end you simply cannot imagine. You could never of yourself find this road or reach your journey's end.[1]

[1]*Dark Night*, bk 2:16.

112

We would do well to balance our reading of the night of the spirit, its flights of poetic rhetoric, with a homely letter addressed to a lady penitent. When it comes to instructing an individual undergoing the night – in what degree we do not know and it is irrelevant – we find John completely and robustly down to earth. In this letter he goes straight to the root of the anxiety and distress she has described to him. He asks the lady what she really wants, what she expects the service of God to consist in? He answers for her:

> Simply in abstaining from evil, keeping God's commandments and doing his work as well as we can. When you do this, what need have you to seek here and there for other instructions, other lights, other consolations, in which ordinarily lurk many snares and dangers for the spiritual person, who is deceived and deluded by her own self-love and insights: her own operations lead her astray.
>
> It is a great grace from God when he so darkens and impoverishes the soul that the senses cannot deceive it. And that it may not go astray it has nothing to do but to walk in the beaten path of the law of God and of the Church, living solely by faith, dim and true, in certain hope and perfect charity, looking for all its blessings in heaven; living here as a pilgrim, a beggar, an exile, an orphan, desolate, possessing nothing and looking for everything from God . . .[1]

[1]Letter to Doña Juana Pedraca.

11

The Summit

So John brings us through the dark night to the summit of the mountain. 'And on the mountain nothing.' The dark night has burnt away all egotism from the heart leaving it a pure receptivity for God. Whether this is experienced as a vast emptiness and longing for him or as fulness and possession makes no difference. Throughout this study we have carefully distinguished between the basic facts underlying John's teaching from what is circumstantial, particularly certain possible psychological reactions in spiritual persons. We have cautiously refused to base our understanding on his descriptions of what such and such a state is *like*, that is, how it is *consciously experienced* by an individual. And so it is now, when we come to the state of transforming union or spiritual marriage. John indeed gives reign to his poetic genius in eloquent descriptions of what it is *like* for the bride (we shall use this title now for it has its full significance) especially when there is an overwhelming awareness of that union, which John calls union of the faculties. Nevertheless what it is *like* must have as many variations as there are persons who attain this state. John reminds us more than once that the experience must, of its very nature, elude all precision of thought, all description. It is ineffable for it is God himself. Further we must bear in mind that similar psychological effects can accompany much lower states; even more they can be present in all sorts of human conditions that have nothing directly to do with God. Deep, pure aridity of the dark night can, on the psychological level, seem identical with the aridity, indifference and spiritual apathy of the heedless person – but a world separates them.

We must therefore look for what is the essence of union, or rather the essential 'quality' of the person in the state of union. What *must* be true of her no matter what her psychological repercussions? Total receptivity means total selflessness and this means that God is truly all in this heart. There is no ego on the summit of the mountain, only the honour and glory of God. This must be understood literally. John has laboured to show us how to surrender the whole of ourselves to the Lord, all the powers of soul and body, memory, understanding and will, interior and exterior senses, the desires of spirit and sense. This is done progressively both as a generous and unremitting effort on our part and by the divine enablement and purgation. Now it is truly accomplished; it has happened. The bride has no desires of the will, no acts of understanding, neither object nor occupation of any kind which she does not refer wholly to God, together with all her desires. We may want this to happen, we may, and indeed must, aim at it; but rarely, says John, is it an actual fact; rarely is a life totally God's. The true bride however is 'taken up' with God, absorbed with him. She is all love. All her activities are love, all her strength and energies are concentrated in love. Love is most truly her sole occupation whatever else she is doing. Like the wise merchant in our Lord's parable she has gladly squandered everything for the supreme treasure, the whole purpose and fulfilment of human being in which lies the honour and glory of God. She is never after her own will, her own gratification, nor is she merely following her own inclinations. She is never engaged in anything that is in the slightest degree alien to him. Her mind is occupied in considering what he wants of her, what will most serve him; her will is in desiring him alone: 'My sole occupation is love.' Here is complete loss of self-love (which we have termed the ego), here is a transcendence that has reached its term, is joined now for ever to what it belongs to. They who truly love are willing to make shipwreck of themselves in order to gain the one they love.[1] The bride has disregarded herself, been profligate not in fits and starts but over long years of patient endurance. Of set purpose she has done this, with steadfast resolution: a labour of faith and undaunted hope which now attains all it hoped for.

The bride lives in light, surrounded by it, penetrated by it from every angle. Because it is unimpeded, naked, full, circumambient, it is essentially formless, like an atmosphere. For most of us light can get at us here and there, now from this angle, now from that, and more persistently as we progress. But with the bride the inflow of light is total. She always sees God, always loves him in the multiple concrete demands of every day. She is never 'not there', never unprepared. Here is real solid virtue; a habit that is the effect of great constant love. 'I do always the things that please him.' Hers is inviolable strength, not as from herself, for she remains poor and weak as well she knows, but from the God who possesses her and communicates to her his own strength. She lives by his life, his virtue, his wisdom, his love; hence her utter security. The bride can never be wrested from this absolute safety. She has chosen to abandon all for his sake, to lose her very self and live in deep solitude. So now God assumes full care of her, holds her in his arms, feeds her with all good things and takes her into his deepest secrets. He is now her sole guide and works in her directly and immediately all the time. She is entirely under the influence of the Holy Spirit, moved by him and him alone. As John expresses it in scholastic terms, she is endowed with the fulness of the gifts of the Holy Spirit. She is never, never alone for she always does what pleases the Father.[2]

Does not the figure of Jesus inevitably rise before the eyes of our mind? Have we not described precisely what the gospels reveal of Jesus, the Father's beloved? John of the Cross speaks of the deification of the human person, becoming God, being equal as it were to God. How this can be misinterpreted

[1] *Canticle*, st. 28–9.
[2] ibid. st. 34–5.

unless we keep our eyes on Jesus. John has bidden us do this throughout. Jesus is a receptivity so absolute that he is true God of true God; the Father is able to communicate himself to him in fulness. In his humble mortal life, a life like ours, of hours and days, he sees the Father always and everywhere and lives out of that vision. Thus it is that 'he who sees me sees the Father'. It is the Father who speaks through him, who acts through his total obedience and receptivity, because he *can* speak and act through him. Jesus is truly human because he is divine. He lives God-life humanly. He is God's human existence.

Human being only becomes what it is when it is handed over, given up and lost in the incomprehensible mystery of God. In Jesus this open-ended, self-abandoning, self-transcendent being has attained its goal, that towards which by its very essence it strives, and it is to him we come with our own empty infinitude for completion in him.[1] We do not expect our life's experience to be difference from his. He was as totally possessed by his Father in his earthly life when he worked and ate and slept, when he wept with pain and frustration, when he felt abandoned and desolate on the cross, as he now is in glory. The servant is not above his master. As the Father communicates himself fully to Jesus, so Jesus communicates himself fully to his bride – all that the Father has given me – ALL, literally. The bride therefore shares most profoundly in Jesus' salvific work of bringing everyone to the Father. 'One single act of pure love is of greater potency than all other works put together', and here is, not one single act, but a life of love.

[1] cf Karl Rahner, 'On the theology of the incarnation', *Theological Investigations*, vol. IV (1974).